Literature in Perspective

General Editor: Kenneth Grose

Shelley

Literature in Perspective

Shelley

Gillian Carey

Evans Brothers Limited London

Published by Evans Brothers Limited
Montague House, Russell Square, London, W.C.1.

First published 1975

Set in 11 on 12 point Bembo and printed in Great Britain by
The Garden City Press Limited, Letchworth, Hertfordshire
SG6 1JS

237 44820 3 cased   PRA 4352

237 44821 1 limp

Literature in Perspective

Reading is a pleasure; reading great literature is a great pleasure, which can be enhanced by increased understanding, both of the actual words on the page and of the background to those words, supplied by a study of the author's life and circumstances. Criticism should try to foster understanding in both aspects.

Unfortunately for the intelligent layman and young reader alike, recent years have seen critics of literature (particularly academic ones) exploring slender ramifications of meaning, exposing successive levels of association and reference, and multiplying the types of ambiguity unto seventy times seven.

But a poet is 'a man speaking to men', and the critic should direct his efforts to explaining not only what the poet says, but also what sort of man the poet is. It is our belief that it is impossible to do the first without doing the second.

Literature in Perspective, therefore, aims at giving a straightforward account of literature and of writers—straightforward both in content and in language. Critical jargon is as far as possible avoided; any terms that must be used are explained simply; and the constant preoccupation of the authors of the series is to be lucid.

It is our hope that each book will be easily understood, that it will adequately describe its subject without pretentiousness so that the intelligent reader who wants to know about Donne or Keats or Shakespeare will find enough in it to bring him up to date on critical estimates.

Even those who are well read, we believe, can benefit from a lucid exposition of what they may have taken for granted, and perhaps—dare it be said?—not fully understood.

K. H. G.

Shelley

Shelley is the least read of major English poets. The blame for this lies largely with T. S. Eliot and F. R. Leavis, whose disparagements, now almost half a century old, widely influenced a whole generation of English teachers. Eliot considered Shelley 'almost a blackguard', and complained that his ideas were adolescent. Dr. Leavis found the poetry too abstract for his taste, and wished Shelley had been more 'concrete', like Keats. That was Keats's feeling, too: 'load every rift of your subject with ore', he cautioned the older poet. However, Shelley's finest work is of a totally distinct kind from Keats's finest, and only narrowness will decry either.

A 'passionate apprehension of abstract ideas' is, as Eliot noted, Shelley's distinguishing feature. But this is not synonymous with vagueness, or with vaguely invoked 'Platonism'. He is the poet of the mind, and the mind's self-searchings. States of mind repeatedly figure as the protagonists in his poetic narratives. The ego and the super-ego relentlessly engage. In the last resort, Shelley knows, the oppressors and tyrants are not conveniently distinguishable public figures, but parts of oneself. In this he foreshadows Freud and later psychoanalysts, as he does in his rejection of guilt and punishment. But he distrusts easy answers, including psychoanalytical ones. He sees that society warps and corrupts men, and then punishes the wickedness that it has created. Yet he believed, too, that what we call 'evil' (like what we call 'creativity' or 'power') is part of a primitive, irresistible energy that links man with the wild and terrible in nature. The breadth, vigour and wariness of Shelley's intelligence could be accounted adolescent only by a critic intent on censure rather than truth. It seems likely that Eliot's prudery and devout Anglicanism prevented him from reaching an objective estimate of this adulterous and atheistic writer.

Nor will Dr. Leavis's claim that Shelley lacked self-knowledge bear much scrutiny. His letters and poems show him unusually alert to the risk of self-deception. One of his constant preoccupations is the running battle between the assertion of self and the need to lose one's self in someone else, or in an idea or activity. He was aware of the contradictions in the middle-class revolutionary's position, and he worked out with honesty and seriousness the implications of relinquishing conventional religion and conventional marriage.

Regrettably the opinions of Eliot and Leavis have distracted attention from more scholarly attempts to discover what Shelley was investigating in his poetry—for instance, Desmond King-Hele's account of the scientific basis of much of Shelley's speculation. The present study draws on this and other modern work, and it provides an introduction to Shelley's life, thought and writing (explaining mythological, political and personal references as they occur), which should allow the reader to find his way to the more rewarding parts of the Poetical Works while retaining a sense of their total context. The result will be an acquaintance with one of the most refreshing and friendly minds, and one of the greatest lyric gifts, English literature can offer. 'I like to hear thee talk, friend Shelley; I see thee art very deep', said Dr. Pope, a Quaker acquaintance. It was, after all, more intelligent than calling him a blackguard, or regretting he wasn't Keats.

G.C.

Contents

The Author

Gillian Carey, M.A., is Tutor in English at Manchester College, Oxford.

Acknowledgements

The author and publishers are indebted to the following for permission to use illustrations: The National Portrait Gallery for the portrait of Shelley by Miss Amelia Curran, the Curators of the Bodleian Library for the pen-sketch from *The Revolt of Islam* and the miniature of Mary Shelley by Reginald Eastman, Shelley's sketches from *The Mask of Anarchy* reproduced by permission of The Huntington Library, San Marino, California, and the cover photograph of Shelley drawn by Mary Shelley by courtesy of the Humanities Research Centre, The University of Texas at Austin.

I

Shelley's Life in England

Percy Bysshe Shelley was born on 4 August, 1792, at Field Place, near Horsham, Sussex. In July 1822, a month short of his thirtieth birthday, he was drowned when his boat sank off the Italian coast near Leghorn. Boating was his favourite pastime and drowning was a death which attracted him in a number of his poems. Even his widow, Mary, could say afterwards that there was a 'sublime fitness' in his fate. Indeed Shelley's life has seemed to literary critics, to those who knew him, even to Shelley himself, like a piece of fiction. There has been a tendency to make a heroic tale out of it. The type of hero has varied—tyrant-hater, atheistical seducer, 'ineffectual angel' (Matthew Arnold), 'herd-abandoned deer' (Shelley himself). There were aspects of his life accounting for all these conflicting views. But a sense of its consistency is created by certain repeated patterns.

On several occasions his life followed books he was reading; he showed a desire both for mentors and for disciples; though he longed for a settled home he was always restlessly travelling; his love for each of the three girls he wanted to marry was opposed by parents; his household usually contained more than one woman; a series of enthusiastic friendships ended in revulsion or disappointment; his first wife and a sister-in-law both committed suicide; he was deprived of two of his children by order of the Lord Chancellor, and he lost three children by death (four if we count another sister-in-law's child, who was part of his household for some years, five if we count an adopted daughter who never lived with him). Almost all these repeated patterns are ones of distress, but there were counteracting positives in his life: his love of liberty, his tolerance, his passion for reading, his combination of generosity, asceticism and extravagance, and of rational argument allied to a keen spiritual sense. He showed considerable resilience to his frequent illnesses and the appalling events that beset him.

Shelley's childhood gives few hints of the storms to come. He was the first child of a generally well-regarded Whig M.P., Timothy Shelley, and grandson of a wealthy if eccentric baronet, Sir Bysshe Shelley. He could expect a fine estate and a seat in Parliament as his inheritance. His four sisters provided a captive audience for his stories; his brother, youngest of the family, gave him no competition. The lack of boys of his own age to play with may have made it more difficult to adjust to school, first Syon House Academy at the age of ten and then Eton at fourteen. His cousin, Tom Medwin, declared that he 'knew nothing whatever of either the technique or the ethics of giving or taking punishment'. Another schoolfellow remembers him 'rolling on the floor when flogged, not from the pain, but from a sense of the indignity'. Here may have been some of the origins of his hatred of tyrants and retributive punishment, his readiness to ally himself with the oppressed, his horror of shame and degradation.

It seems that at least towards the end of his career at Eton he was fairly well accepted. Still there are stories of 'Shelley-baiting', and his friend Thomas Love Peacock recalls that in after-life Shelley spoke of those days with a feeling of abhorrence unparalleled except when he spoke of the Lord Chancellor who deprived him of his children. A feeling of persecution recurred throughout his life, finding expression at least once in hallucination.

Shelley was very quick to learn and had a remarkable memory, but it seems that schoolwork, mainly Latin and Greek, did not fire his imagination. For this he turned to science and romances. He had been entranced at Syon House by a visiting lecturer, Adam Walker, who demonstrated both the telescope and the microscope. Later, scientific instruments were amongst Shelley's most treasured possessions and it says a lot for his generosity that he once pawned his microscope to give ten pounds to a totally unknown and destitute old man. Meanwhile he indulged in various scientific experiments, more or less perilous, involving poison, gunpowder, and the electrification of a tom-cat. Fortunately he avoided self-destruction, though the interest in poisons and combustibles continued. Science satisfied his craving for the rational, for the observation of cause and effect. But it was also allied to his delight in the marvellous which he fed on a diet of 'horrid' romances 'till', as he said in a letter written when he was fifteen, 'I fancy myself a Character'.

The other influence of importance during his schooldays was Dr. James Lind, a physician to the king, living in Windsor. He was a radical, a friend of James Watt (of steam-engine fame), had travelled as far as China and Iceland, and was interested in antiquities, printing and astronomy. In short he was, according to Shelley, 'exactly what an old man ought to be, free, calm-spirited, full of benevolence and even of youthful ardour'. It was probably Dr. Lind who introduced Shelley to William Godwin's *Political Justice* and so, indirectly, to his future father-in-law and financial burden.

Shelley's first published work, a prose romance, *Zastrozzi*, was written while he was still at Eton and appeared in March 1810. It displays his love of the appalling and a reassuring interest in regular meals. The characters' extreme emotions result in much fainting by the good and cursing and stabbing by the bad. Backgrounds consist of stupendous scenery and sofas. There is a touching innocence about it. Beautiful passive heroine and beautiful dynamic villainess share what seems a modest requirement for good looks—they both have a 'symmetrical form'—and, after the wickedest of schemings, villain and villainess part, 'warned by the lateness of the hour to separate'. *Zastrozzi* was followed into print in September of the same year by *Original Poetry by Victor and Cazire* ('downright scribble' a reviewer called it), to which his favourite sister, Elizabeth, contributed.

This was also the period of disappointment in his first love affair—with his cousin, Harriet Grove. She at first encouraged him, but later became alarmed at his unconventional views. Their engagement was broken off by her father before Shelley went up to University College, Oxford, in the autumn of 1810. His anger and disappointment at this rejection, and his belief that the neighbour she subsequently married in 1811 was 'a clod of earth', in whose company her 'fine capabilities' would 'moulder', all contributed to his sense of persecution when he came into conflict with the college authorities and with his father.

At first, however, failure in an adolescent love affair does not seem to have clouded his initial term at Oxford. Most of our information about this comes from the life-long friend he met there, Thomas Jefferson Hogg. Hogg's *Life of Shelley* has to be viewed with suspicion since he trims and exaggerates for the sake of a good story, but his account of Oxford days transmits a sense of excitement and promise, and an admiration for Shelley which lives through the sceptical humour of his later phrase-making.

They met over an argument at dinner in the college hall about the respective merits of Italian and German literature, an argument so eager that they did not notice that they had been left alone at table, but one based on almost total ignorance, as first Shelley and then Hogg confessed when they adjourned to Hogg's rooms. Indeed it soon appeared to Hogg that literature and language were not then Shelley's prime enthusiasm. Classical learning was 'merely the study of words and phrases, of the names of things'. Far better study things themselves through the physical sciences. This Hogg found Shelley was doing to the detriment of his expensively decorated room. Noxious smells, alarming experiments and enthusiastic accounts of the possible benefits to mankind of scientific advance—air travel, electricity, water in the desert—testified to his scientific curiosity and idealism. Fascinated by the jumble of his room and the eloquence of his talk, but wary for his own safety, Hogg drew Shelley into such harmless pursuits as long walks in the neighbouring countryside. Shelley behaved characteristically, making paper boats to sail on convenient ponds, buying milk for an apparently abandoned little girl (a possible candidate for a recurrent scheme of Shelley's for adopting and educating an uncorrupted female child), or seizing a baby on Magdalen Bridge and demanding of its mother,

'Will your baby tell us anything about pre-existence, Madam?'
Startled though she was, Shelley's gentleness was so evident that
she apparently felt no apprehension for the child's safety.

Hogg presents Shelley as a contradictory character, pursuing
scientific enquiry, but being inclined to an almost religious
veneration; fascinated by logic, but moved by a strong spiritual
sense; distrusting words but reading voraciously. Apart from
benevolence what seems to underlie the contradictions is an
eager optimism, never spelt out by Hogg, but suggested by his
accounts of Shelley's scientific speculations, and interest in children,
and even by the characteristic sound, vibrating in Hogg's memory,
of Shelley's running footsteps in the quad. Shelley had faith in the
future.

And Shelley meant to help shape the future. One of the ways
to do that was to clear the air of religious cant, to bring funda-
mental questions of belief into the open to be discussed freely and
honestly. Hence *The Necessity for Atheism*. The title suggests a
thorough-going manifesto. In fact it is a brief, reasonable pamphlet, actuated, the author tells us, by 'a love of truth'. It asserts
not that there is no God, but that the existence of God cannot be
proved. (Indeed Shelley himself believed, as he wrote to Hogg in
January 1811, that 'some vast intellect animates Infinity'.) Belief
not being an act of volition, it is no crime to disbelieve; and
acknowledgement of the truth can never harm society. He asks
readers who can discover flaws in his arguments to offer their
views methodically to the public. To this end he sent copies to
heads of colleges, professors and bishops. Admittedly at this
period Shelley shows a desire to shock as is evident from two
publications late in 1810—a second novel, *St. Irvyne*, and a
burlesque poem, *Posthumous fragments of Margaret Nicholson*,
supposedly by a woman who had tried to murder George III.

Also Shelley must have known that at a period when daily
attendance at college chapel was compulsory and membership
of the Church of England a requirement for residence in the
university his pamphlet would not be looked on with favour.
Nevertheless it is regrettable that none of the senior members of
the university made any attempt to discuss his views rationally

with the young agnostic. Instead, half an hour after Shelley had scattered some copies in a bookshop window, the Professor of Poetry ordered the bookseller to burn them and informed the Master of University College. When Shelley refused to deny that he was the author of the anonymous leaflet he was expelled, not for atheism but for 'contumacy' in refusing to answer questions. 'If', as Hogg said, 'his good star had led him to a college where he would have been treated frankly, kindly and handsomely, the result of his academic residence would have been altogether different and more beneficial.' In fact his career might have been what he had anticipated—that of a politician rather than a poet. As it was, he and Hogg, who voluntarily confessed to being implicated in the project, left together on the London coach on 26 March, 1811.

Disappointed at this wanton throwing away of opportunity, their fathers were anxious to separate the two young men and in April Hogg went to study law in York. Shelley father and son understood each other less and less, Timothy eventually dealing tactlessly through a lawyer and feeling wounded by his son's offer to give up his right to the family estate. Though his father made him an allowance and he returned for a time to Field Place, Shelley felt persecuted for his beliefs, and lonely without Hogg. He met Leigh Hunt, and a thirty-year-old schoolteacher who for about a year became 'the sister of his soul'. More importantly he encountered a school friend of his sisters, Harriet Westbrook, who became his wife. She was sixteen and the daughter of a retired, well-to-do coffee-house keeper. A month before eloping to Edinburgh where he married her on 28 August, 1811, he was writing to Hogg that he was not in love. Three weeks before, he wrote that she looked to him to rescue her from 'persecution' at school over their friendship, and that 'gratitude and admiration all demanded that he should love her for ever'. Ten days before, he wrote that he was determined on marriage. This was a surprise, for he disapproved of marriage. 'For God's sake', he had once remarked, 'read the marriage service before you think of allowing an amiable beloved female to submit to such degradation.' However he came to feel that the woman had to make a disproportionate sacrifice in entering into a free union. Harriet had sent him an anti-free love novel to read, and in any case already in *St. Irvyne* he had presented a hero and heroine who waived their distaste for marriage for the sake of 'procuring moral expediency'.

In the long term the marriage was disastrous since it made reconciliation with Shelley's father impossible, at once creating financial burdens and cutting off the source of money. Far worse, its breakdown three years later led to Harriet's suicide, to Shelley's separation from their children, and to his guilt and anguish. In the short term, however, it produced a good deal of happiness and was the period of Shelley's most active political involvement. Hogg, who immediately joined the Shelleys in Edinburgh, found Harriet pretty, neat, well-read, not interested in religion but interested in morality. In many ways she must have seemed a suitable wife for Shelley. His father thought otherwise and when Shelley informed him of the match in a rather arrogant note, stopped his allowance.

Shelley's finances were saved by a sympathetic uncle, Captain Pilfold (who had earlier intervened on his behalf), and the three friends went to York for Hogg to continue his legal studies. Clearly Shelley envisaged coming into a fortune at some point, presumably when he was twenty-one, for he was soon promising a share of it to the 'sister of his soul' Elizabeth Hitchener, with whom he resumed his correspondence. Hogg too would benefit. Soon however he proved himself to be unworthy of such trust. When Shelley was away trying to come to some accommodation with his father (partly through the intervention of his father's Whig political patron, the Duke of Norfolk) Hogg tried, unsuccessfully, to seduce Harriet. For all his ironical tone in after years, Hogg followed Shelley into love with both his wives, having already been in love with the idea of Elizabeth Shelley (whom he probably never saw). He eventually married the last woman Shelley was drawn to, Jane Williams.

Theoretically, Shelley was prepared to share his wife with his friend but Harriet was averse to being shared: 'I attach little value to the monopoly of exclusive cohabitation', Shelley wrote to Hogg, but he was bound to have regard for what 'Harriet cherishes as a prejudice interwoven with the fibres of her being'. To Hogg after separating from him, he may have written more in sorrow than in anger, still slightly hysterically protesting love for him, eventually declining a duel when Hogg tried to elicit a violent reaction. But to Elizabeth Hitchener he revealed that he felt betrayed by his friend and disillusioned with human nature. After all, Harriet had been left in Hogg's protection: 'Human nature appears so depraved . . . virtue has lost one of its defenders—vice has gained a proselyte.'

Before Shelley returned from Sussex Harriet gained a chaperone in her thirty-year-old sister, Eliza, who now took over the management of the household. Hogg paints a repulsive picture of her, always brushing her hair, but with a face 'like rice boiled in dirty water', and he attributes the deterioration of the relationship between Harriet and Shelley to Eliza's presence. It was plain, he said, that Shelley had been superseded. It might have been more true to say that Hogg had been replaced in the threesome when Harriet reported his approaches. Certainly at first Shelley considered that although Eliza was prejudiced, her prejudices were not unvanquishable and he was quite ready to let her take over the day-to-day household arrangements. With brief intervals she lived with them almost to the end of Shelley's married life with Harriet. But by the time she eventually left in April 1814 Shelley hated her. Now, however, the three decamped to Keswick without telling Hogg.

There were two good reasons for going to Keswick. Firstly Shelley wanted to see the Lakes and the Lake Poets, Wordsworth, Coleridge and Southey. Secondly the Duke of Norfolk had a house in that area and he might yet effect a reconciliation with Shelley's father. In the event, the only poet they met was Southey. But a week with the Duke—they spent their last guinea getting there—resulted in the paternal £200 a year being recontinued.

Disappointed in Southey's luke-warm politics, Shelley discussed his ideas in letters to Elizabeth Hitchener, whom he continued to idealise in spite of her warning to 'see me more as I *really am*', and to William Godwin. Discovering that Godwin was not dead, as he had supposed, he wrote introducing himself: 'I am young—I am ardent in the cause of philanthropy and truth.' It was, he said, on reading *Political Justice* that he had realised he had been living merely in a world of romance, and that he had 'duties to perform'. Shelley showed a blithe confidence: 'My plan is that of resolving to lose no opportunity to disseminate truth and happiness.' Meanwhile he was hoping for a co-worker in the dissemination of truth. Elizabeth Hitchener should come and live with them; making money wasn't important; there would be enough chairs, beds and food for them all. 'Let us,' he wrote to her a little later, 'mingle our identities inseparably, and burst upon tyrants with the accumulated impetuosity of our acquirements and resolutions.' Shelley realised that other people reading his letters to Elizabeth might think him a bit mad, and he toned down his style in his letters to Godwin: 'I hope in the course of our communication to acquire that sobriety of spirit which is the characteristic of true heroism.' He wanted to be modest but useful. Godwin was interested but wary: 'As far as I can yet penetrate your character,' he wrote in March 1812, 'I conceive it to exhibit an extraordinary assemblage of lovely qualities, not without considerable defects. The defects do and always have arisen chiefly from this source—that you are still very young, and that in certain essential respects, you do not sufficiently perceive that you are so.' Southey had put the same criticism more depressingly in saying that Shelley would think as he did when he got to his age. This was emphatically what Shelley did not want. He had no wish to be Southey's disciple. He was also rather disillusioned with Keswick and the people there. He speaks of 'debauched servants of great houses', and the contamination of manufacturers who had 'crept into the peaceful vale and deformed the loveliness of Nature with human taint'. Besides, the neighbours were hostile, looking on his experiments with hydrogen gas with suspicion. The story of an attack on Shelley by a would-be robber may have been merely a reflection of his sense of local hostility. But a move was indicated, and Shelley decided to visit Ireland.

He had become increasingly concerned about the oppression of the people there. An unsuccessful rebellion in 1798 had been brutally put down by Lord Castlereagh, and the Act of 1801 uniting the Irish and English Parliaments had not brought peace. Only the Protestant propertied minority were represented. There was therefore continuing agitation for Catholic emancipation. Shelley was perhaps more interested in the repeal of the Act of Union. He felt that Catholic emancipation on its own would benefit only the small number of Catholics who were prosperous enough to be entitled to vote. But separation from England might lead to the liberation of the mass of the people, who were miserably poor. Here was a situation in which tyranny could be opposed and truth disseminated. On 2 February, 1812, the Shelleys and Eliza Westbrook sailed for Ireland.

Perhaps encouraged by the Duke of Norfolk, long a champion of Catholic emancipation, Shelley had already been composing *An Address to the Irish People*. This pamphlet was simply expressed and cheaply printed, in order to be accessible to ordinary people, and Shelley and Harriet helped to distribute copies in the streets of Dublin soon after their arrival. In it Shelley expressed himself the friend of the Irish people, advocated the repeal of the Act of Union, Catholic emancipation, and indeed entire religious toleration, and opposed all forms of violence. The plea for toleration is based on one of the arguments of the *Necessity for Atheism*—belief cannot be willed. Therefore what makes a man good is not what he believes, which is involuntary, but his goodwill towards others. The best religion is therefore the one which makes men most virtuous.

The Irish Catholics are right to desire emancipation, but they too should be tolerant, because 'Nothing on earth is infallible'. A letter to Elizabeth Hitchener shows that Shelley really wanted to 'shake Catholicism at its basis'. The audience at a meeting he addressed applauded him when he advocated Catholic emancipation, but hissed him when he got on to religion. Yet much of what he had to say would not be amiss in a sermon—they must be 'calm, mild, deliberate, patient'; they must 'never do evil that good may come'; they should read and discuss, form associations, but avoid mobs. Reform in Ireland might be one step towards a better society. It starts with the reform of the individual. Shelley's advice to the Irish could be summed up in the words of the Sermon on the Mount: 'Be ye perfect.' It is no surprise to find Shelley writing in a letter the same month: 'I have often thought that the moral sayings of Jesus Christ might be very useful if selected from the mystery and immorality which surrounds them.'

Favourable notice was taken of his enlightenment—'To this gentleman Ireland is much indebted, for selecting her as the theatre of his first attempts in this holy work of human regeneration,' said the Dublin *Weekly Messenger*. But Shelley's counsels of perfection had little effect. Distressed by the miserable poverty he saw in Dublin, he was also despondent at the ignorance, selfishness, intolerance and lack of support from Catholics. The one lasting friend they made during their seven weeks' stay was a poor, middle-aged seamstress who was also a staunch republican. Shelley chose friends for likemindedness.

From Ireland they moved first to Wales, where they failed to raise the purchase price of the house they wanted, and then to Lynmouth. Here Elizabeth Hitchener joined them in their cramped cottage lodgings, and here *Queen Mab* was begun. Godwin, too, was to visit them, but by the time he arrived they had moved to Ilfracombe and then to Tremadoc in Wales. Their Irish servant, Dan Hill, had been arrested for distributing Shelley's next pamplet, *A Declaration of Rights*. Clearly in those days the assertions: 'Government has no rights; it is a delegation from several individuals for securing their own'; or 'A man has a right to unrestricted liberty of discussion'; or 'No man has a right to monopolise more than he can enjoy; what the rich give to the poor, whilst millions are starving, is not a perfect favour, but an imperfect right'; or 'Every man has a right to a certain degree of leisure and liberty, because it is his duty to attain a certain degree of knowledge', were regarded as dangerously subversive. Some of Shelley's methods of promulgating his beliefs may have been bizarre—entrusting his pamphlets to bottles launched on the sea, or to hot-air balloons—but he was thought to be important enough to be kept under surveillance by government agents. He was known to have corresponded with Sir Francis Burdett, opponent of the recently assassinated Prime Minister, Spencer Percival. A box containing pamphlets sent from Ireland to Elizabeth Hitchener had been opened and a report sent to the Home Secretary.

The Shelleys remained in Wales till the following spring, apart from a six weeks' visit to London in the autumn when he finally met Godwin and his family. There also he resumed his friendship with Hogg and made some new friends; John Newton, an advocate of vegetarianism (Shelley was already a vegetarian); Thomas Hookham, the publisher of *Queen Mab*; and Thomas Love Peacock the novelist.

In Wales Shelley was busy raising funds—he contributed £100 himself—for the completion of an embankment at Tremadoc which was supposed to create good farming land and bring prosperity to the area. At present it produced only distress to the unpaid labourers which Shelley tried to relieve. While he was giving away large and small sums in these ways he was in debt himself and unable to raise enough money for a permanent home. This is the continuing pattern of Shelley's finances—he was always wanting to help others and he consistently failed to live within his income. He tended therefore to leave mixed reactions behind him. Some respected his warm generosity, others resented him because his charity and enthusiasm showed up their meanness and because he was never solvent.

There was enough animosity in Tremadoc for there to be another real or imaginary attack on Shelley, more violent and dramatic than the Keswick episode, this time involving two assaults, firearms and a drawing by Shelley of a 'devil' who tried to kill him. Though a good shot, he failed to wound the 'devil'. Several theories have arisen from the conflicting accounts of the incident: that Shelley was suffering from delusions, that there really was an attack but magnified by Shelley's imagination, that the whole thing was either consciously or semi-consciously engineered by Shelley because he wished to avoid either his creditors in the neighbourhood or the drudgery and frustration of his office work in the embankment enterprise. What is certain is that, once more 'persecuted', Shelley went to Ireland again with Harriet and Eliza Westbrook but without Elizabeth Hitchener who after four months had parted from them in London. At close quarters the 'sister of his soul' had turned into the 'brown demon'. As well as disliking her, he must have felt guilty at having disrupted her life. It would be difficult for her to go back to her father and schoolteaching after having been part of a household consisting of a young poet and three women.

After a holiday in Killarney they returned to London. Here *Queen Mab* was published and Harriet's first child, Ianthe, born. The friendship with the vegetarian Newtons soon included Mrs. Newton's sister Mrs. Boinville and her daughter, Cornelia Turner, with whom Shelley learned Italian. The autumn of 1813 was again spent in travelling, perhaps to escape creditors, to the Lakes, Edinburgh and back to Windsor. Shelley's financial difficulties increased; he raised money on his expectations but supplied Godwin with £1,000; he incurred needless expense in travelling, and ordered a carriage he never paid for. Relations with Harriet deteriorated. Hogg thought her changed when they returned, she seemed intellectually complacent. Shelley increasingly resented Eliza, who took charge of Ianthe. Perhaps it had been under her influence that Harriet insisted on engaging a wet nurse for the baby, much to Shelley's chagrin. All in all Shelley was depressed in the spring of 1814. Increasingly he turned to the Boinvilles till Mrs. Boinville prudently discouraged his growing friendship with Cornelia.

In March as a legal precaution he re-married Harriet according to English law, but she remained at Windsor, while in London Shelley tried to raise loans against his inheritance (urged on by the now financially dependent Godwin). In London he spent his time with the Godwins, including the sixteen-year-old Mary who had just left school. She was Godwin's daughter by his first wife Mary Wollstencraft, author of *A Vindication of the Rights of Woman*. She had died soon after Mary was born, leaving Godwin with a stepdaughter as well, the plain but sensible Fanny

Imlay. His second wife brought him two more stepchildren, Charles and Jane Clairmont (known as Claire). A young son of the second marriage made up the impoverished family. Mary was immediately attractive to Shelley. She had as her parents the authors of two books which had deeply influenced him. She was herself beautiful and intellectual. And she declared her love for him, apparently during a highly emotional visit to her mother's grave.

In theory in favour of free love, Godwin was appalled when Shelley told him of his feelings. He and Mary Wollstencraft had been free to live together if they chose and they married only shortly before their daughter's birth. But now that daughter was breaking up a marriage. Under pressure from the Godwins, Shelley and Mary agreed to stop seeing each other, but Shelley was soon back, pistol in hand and a dose of laudanum inside him. This might have been fatal had not a doctor, the Godwins and Mrs. Boinville kept him walking for hours on end.

Away in Bath at the time of the declaration Harriet, again pregnant, had become alarmed when Shelley's letters suddenly stopped. The news awaiting her when she returned made her very ill, but she behaved with moderation, blaming Mary and hoping that Shelley would get over his infatuation for the designing daughter of Mary Wollstencraft. Shelley naïvely hoped that Harriet could be persuaded to live as a sister with himself and Mary. He still wanted to protect and guide her and care for their children, but he no longer felt they were intellectually compatible, and he now either believed or tried to believe that he had never had any passion for her. It shows an astonishing lack of understanding for someone of Shelley's sensitivity to think for one moment that such an arrangement could be tolerable to Harriet. Perhaps it was an unconscious defensive device to avoid the misery of guilt. Perhaps he really believed that Harriet shared his views on marriage and would be above jealousy. But on the contrary she loved him, was bearing his second child, and had no intention of giving him up.

For several months Shelley had felt trapped in his marriage. Now he was in love, and he genuinely thought Mary his intellectual superior. So on 27 July he eloped for the second time. With them was the adventurous Claire Clairmont, escaping no doubt from the gloomy and distressed Godwin household. They travelled to Switzerland through country fought over in Napoleon's last campaign. They busily kept journals, admired the grandeur of the scenery but were fastidious about foreigners. After six weeks, short of funds, they returned via the Rhine to England where Shelley immediately borrowed £20 from Harriet. The marriage which began so hopefully three years before petered out in wrangles about money.

After their separation they continued to show their concern for each other, proffering advice on health for example, but bitterness soon pervaded this lingering relationship. Shelley, when he could, paid Harriet an allowance, and made good his undertaking to support Godwin, who accepted his money but refused to see him. Shelley was soon in hiding from bailiffs and creditors, and his finances only looked up in the spring of the following year with the death of his grandfather. This enabled him to opt for £1,000 a year immediately, in place of a much larger income after his father's death.

In December 1814 Harriet's son Charles had been born. In February 1815 Mary's first child, born prematurely, had lived less than a fortnight. Hogg, who had joined them in December, was soon vowing love to Mary, who, though not objecting on principle, grew to dislike him. Claire had left the household in May after growing friction with Mary. But after a holiday in Devon and with a settled income Shelley entered one of the most tranquil periods of his life when he took a house near Windsor Park in August 1815. Here he wrote *Alastor* (see Chapter 3). Mary's second child, William, was born in January 1816; Hogg and Peacock were frequent visitors.

New clouds, however, gathered in 1816. Godwin, in dire straits, was pressing Shelley for money. Still believing in Godwin as a philosopher though disillusioned with him as a man and deeply hurt that he refused to meet him, Shelley did what he could. Meanwhile, in London, Claire had contrived to meet the fascinating and notorious Lord Byron, had become his mistress, and now in May diverted Shelley and Mary from intended travels in Italy, persuading them instead to go to Geneva so that she could follow her lover there. Shelley's meeting and friendship with Byron brought intellectual stimulation for Mary too. It was then that she began her famous novel, *Frankenstein*. But it also brought difficulties. Since Byron soon tired of Claire, Shelley became the mediator between them over their daughter, Allegra, born the following January. Byron's admiration for Shelley was constant—'the best, the least selfish man I have ever known'. Shelley's feelings for Byron were mixed: though his powers were great he was 'a slave to the vilest and most vulgar prejudices'. His attitude to life was cynical, to Claire, callous.

Shelley's letters at this time reveal admiration for the Alpine scenery but also a nostalgia for England, excitement over friendship with the most popular and outrageous poet of the day, but also a strong desire for domestic retirement. He commissioned Peacock to find a house for him to return to, and meanwhile look after his household gods: 'They are innocent deities, and their worship is neither sanguinary nor absurd ... The shrines of the Penates are good wood fires, or window frames intertwined with creeping plants; their hymns are the purring of kittens, the hissing of kettles; the long talks over the past and dead; the laugh of children, the warm wind of summer filling the quiet house, and the pelting storm of winter struggling in vain for entrance.'

Shelley never achieved this idyll. On the return to England two tragedies soon followed. The first of these was the suicide of Mary's half-sister, Fanny, who had expected to find employment and a home at the school run by some aunts in Ireland. But the offer was withdrawn, perhaps because the scandal of Mary and Claire's unconventional behaviour rubbed off on her. She now knew too that she was illegitimate, and must have felt a financial burden on Godwin. There seemed no place for Fanny so she quietly travelled to Swansea and took a fatal dose of laudanum in her hotel room. Shelley was deeply shocked. Remorse at not having thought enough about Fanny appears in the short poem he wrote about her:

> Her voice did quiver as we parted,
>> Yet knew I not that heart was broken
> From which it came, and I departed
>> Heeding not the words then spoken.
>> Misery—O Misery,
>> This world is all too wide for thee.

Exactly two months later the body of Harriet Shelley was pulled, swollen, from the Serpentine.

Harriet had always had suicidal tendencies, even when she was perfectly well and happy. We might discount Hogg's spirited account of how, serene and blooming, 'she scattered dismay amongst a quiet party of vegetable eaters, persons who would not slay a shrimp, or extinguish animal life in embryo by eating an egg, by asking, whether they did not feel strongly inclined to kill themselves'. But there had been evidence of an interest in suicide in her letters. After Shelley had left her she had lived mainly at her father's, but the last months of her life are obscure so we cannot know what finally turned the adolescent inclination, smiled at by others, into the lonely act from which even the thought of her children could not restrain her.

Shelley took the news of Harriet's death outwardly calmly though to Peacock he did reveal something of his anguish of mind. His main preoccupation was the tussle over Harriet's children whom the Westbrooks were determined to keep, declaring Shelley an unfit person to have charge of their upbringing because of his atheism and immorality. They brought a suit in Chancery which was only finally settled after eighteen months. As Leigh Hunt put it, he was 'convicted of holding the unpublished opinions which his public teachers at the University had not thought fit to reason him out of'. Whether or not judgment was given against him because of his philosophy rather than his conduct, the Lord Chancellor, Lord Eldon, ruled that the children should be given to guardians approved by the court, that the Westbrooks could visit them often, but Shelley very rarely, though his father, Sir Timothy, could see them when he liked. Once more Shelley felt persecuted for his beliefs. He hated

Lord Eldon, especially since he was afraid that Mary's children might also be taken from him.

Meanwhile his life in Marlow, where he settled with Mary (they married as soon as he was free to do so), was tranquil. A daughter, Clara, was born to them in September 1817; Claire and her baby lived with them. Friends, especially the Leigh Hunts, Hogg and Peacock, visited. While Shelley's depravity was debated in London, he read, wrote, walked, boated, played with the children, and comforted and relieved the distress of poor lacemakers in the district whose trade was in decline. Here ordinary people remembered his kindness with affection long after his death, as did his boatman on Lake Geneva. Several stories of his benevolence date from this time, including one where he was a Good Samaritan to an obviously sick woman he found in a state of collapse on Hampstead Heath. Till he could fetch a doctor, he sought shelter for her at the house of a well-to-do man. 'Sir,' said this responsible citizen, 'your conduct is extraordinary.' 'Sir!' cried Shelley at last, 'I am sorry to say your conduct is not extraordinary; and if my own seems to amaze you, I will tell you something that may amaze you a little more and I hope will frighten you. It is such men as you who madden the spirits of the poor and wretched; and if ever a convulsion comes in this country (which is very probable) recollect what I tell you; you will have your house, that you refuse to put the miserable woman into, burnt over your head.'

Leigh Hunt, who recounted this story later, defended Shelley against the charge in the *Quarterly* that he was shamefully dissolute in his conduct. He gives this account of his life at Marlow:

> He was up early; breakfasted sparingly, wrote his *Revolt of Islam* all morning; went out in his boat or into the woods with some Greek author—or the Bible in his hands; came home to a dinner of vegetables (for he took neither meat nor wine); visited (if necessary) 'the sick and fatherless' whom others gave Bibles to and no help; wrote or studied again, or read to his wife and friends the whole evening; took a crust of bread or a glass of whey for his supper; and went early to bed.

This settled life did not last. A combination of circumstances drove him abroad: financial difficulties brought on by the Chancery suit, and by his aid to Godwin, Claire and her brother Charles, Leigh Hunt and Peacock; increasingly poor health, which called for a warmer climate; the necessity for making some arrangement about Claire's child, Allegra, with Byron in Italy; and his fear of being deprived of his children. So early in 1818 Shelley, Mary, Claire and the children left England for Italy. Shelley never returned. Ahead of him lay four years of travel and temporary homes in Italy, renewed contact with Byron, the deaths of William, Clara and Allegra, the composition of most of the poems by which he is chiefly remembered, new friends in the Gisbornes, Trelawney and Jane and Edward Williams. Williams drowned with him; Trelawney arranged his funeral.

Of his life in England there remained: two children he never saw again; Godwin, past inspiration and present thorn in the flesh; a few friends; three poems of importance, *Queen Mab*, *Alastor* and *The Revolt of Islam*—and the memory of Harriet. Mary may have been better suited to Shelley intellectually but Peacock for one left a strong affirmation of Harriet's worth:

> I feel it due to the memory of Harriet to state my most decided conviction that her conduct as a wife was as pure, as true, as absolutely faultless as that of any who for such conduct are held most in honour. If they mixed in society she adorned it; if they lived in retirement she was satisfied; if they travelled she enjoyed the change of scene.

Harriet may have disappointed Shelley, but Shelley also disappointed Harriet, not simply in deserting her but in becoming it seemed to her less ardent for political action, more concerned with self. He had withdrawn from immediate involvement—no more Dublin pamphleteering, no more Welsh embankments, no longer the directness or the fervour of the poem he dedicated to her, *Queen Mab*.

2

Queen Mab

Though Shelley was not yet twenty-one when he published *Queen Mab* (1813) his concerns remained the same until his death. The later modifications in his thought are already inherent in *Queen Mab* and a look at these changes reveals both the underlying unity of purpose in his poetry, and the growing flexibility in attitude dictated by his desire for social regeneration. *Queen Mab* deserves study too because it was here that Shelley proved himself one of those poets who are 'unacknowledged legislators of the world'. Indeed he could almost be called an acknowledged legislator since *Queen Mab*, for the radical followers of Robert Owen, became a trumpet-call of the Labour movement. Though Shelley's first edition consisted of only 250 copies for private distribution, there were at least fourteen cheap pirated editions in the next twenty years. For a generation it was his most widely-read work until the anthologists popularised his lyrics, and rendered Shelley 'safe'—a word-musician with ideas appealing to adolescents. In fact even his lyrics mostly relate to the basic concerns of *Queen Mab*, or to ideas that are implicit in Shelley's characteristic imagery.

Shelley boldly proclaims *Queen Mab* 'a philosophical poem, with notes'. Probably most of it was written during 1812, the year of the retreat from Moscow—enough to impress the horrors of war on the least sensitive mind—and the year which saw, at home, the imprisonment of Leigh Hunt and his brother, for publishing an attack on the Prince Regent, the imprisonment of Cobbett, for writing against paper money, and the Frame-Breaking Bill, resulting from the Luddite disturbances. This bill, unsuccessfully opposed by Byron in his maiden speech in the

House of Lords, made the destruction of machinery a capital offence. Shelley and Harriet contributed to a fund for the orphans of seventeen men hanged at York. During this period too Shelley was, on Godwin's advice, reading history, 'that record of crimes and misery' as Shelley called it. He was also engaged in trying to raise money for the Tremadoc embankment.

In this international and national climate Shelley wrote *Queen Mab* in order to present a philosophical system, largely derived from Godwin's *Political Justice*. He put forward his views of man's past, and its legacy, the present evils that prevented man from reaching a state of peace and happiness. This state, Shelley felt, must be man's eventual destiny. If he couldn't, at twenty, change the course of history, he could at least strike a verbal blow or two for freedom. His theory is deterministic. That is, he believes that instead of a Creator there is a law of necessity which prevails throughout the material universe. Cause and effect follow each other inevitably. Clearly this allows little scope for man's free will, so Shelley's optimism about the future is some-what inconsistent.

The fiction he used to convey his ideas was an aerial chariot ride through the universe to the temple of Queen Mab, and a series of lessons about the past, present and future given by the Queen (a fairy) to the spirit of Ianthe (a mortal). After a brief dedication to Harriet, his 'purer mind', the poem opens with a picture of Ianthe sleeping so peacefully that at first sight she might be dead. The purity of her soul is represented by her whiteness; she is 'breathing marble', her hair curls like ivy tendrils 'around a marble column', her blue veins 'steal like streams along a field of snow'. It might be said that these comparisons are merely decorative—Shelley just likes describing blue veins or, later, the similar effect of Ianthe's eyelids, so fine that they scarcely hide her blue eyes. They are, however, highly character-istic of Shelley. Artists reveal themselves in their 'inessential' de-tails no less than in their most studied effects. What Shelley is really attracted by here is the apparently dead being actually alive, by the life (blue veins or blue eyes) which lies just below the obvious surface. In a similar way streams in snow are always lower than the surface of the snow, the flowing water being as it were the life of crystalline water. This collection of similes is an early inexplicit example of Shelley's pre-occupation with the essences within external forms. It also shows that he is a more precise visual poet than he may at first seem.

The simile introducing the fairy chariot which is to carry Ianthe's spirit on its celestial jaunt suggests the link between the past (with its records of crimes and misery) and the future. This is the basis of the poem's thought, with its pessimism about man's state, and its optimism about his possible regeneration. The noise of the chariot is like 'the wondrous strain/That round a lonely ruin swells/Which the enthusiast hears at evening'. At first the sound is softer than 'the west wind's sigh'. Six years later, in *Ode to the West Wind*, Shelley will seek to be identified with the regenerative west wind itself, and with the lyre 'whose strings the genii of the breezes sweep'. To make the future better than the ruinous past there needs to be a sensitive, pure enthusiast. This is what Shelley later sees as the function of the poet.

The fairy descends from the chariot and bids the soul of Ianthe arise. It is the 'perfect semblance of its bodily frame' as it stands 'immortal amid ruin'. Shelley is obviously fascinated by the inter-relation of soul and body. They share the 'same marks of identity', but whereas the soul longs for a 'sempiternal heritage', the body is 'the unwilling sport of circumstance and passion'. The ambiguity of 'unwilling' ('without a will' or 'against its will') suggests that Shelley really does find it difficult to view body and soul independently. At death the body is like 'a worn-out machine' but it is also part of a natural process, it 'rots'. This is the first indication in the poem of Shelley's rather ambivalent attitude to machines which we shall see more of later. Queen Mab explains why Ianthe has been singled out for a revelation which is both a reward and an inspiration to further spiritual endeavour. It is because her spirit has dived deep and soared high that she is chosen. The diving motif ties in with the notion of downward exploration so frequent in Shelley and other Romantic poets. It suggests a real shift in the way man's moral endeavour was envisaged as compared to earlier views. Previously it was seen as an upward process, linked to the idea of a chain of being. Desire for excellence was, quite literally, aspiration. However, as scientific discovery began to question the idea that 'man superior walks/Amid the glad creation', and as scepticism about the orthodox God increased, man had to review his position.

The new position was at once more companionable, since there was no longer such an absolute dividing line between him and the rest of creation (hence perhaps Shelley's vegetarianism), but also more lonely, since he was no longer part of a chosen species enjoying a special relationship with the creator. This also means that the idea of the heroic must change; conquest and power are bound to become suspect. The fact that Wordsworth could write his epic poem (*The Prelude*) about the growth of his own mind, and expect people to read it, is a sign of the rift between this and the preceding period. Only madmen would have done that previously. The age of psychology is not far off.

The chariot moves off to the accompaniment of 'speechless music', suggestive of the music of the spheres (and also indicative of a distrust of words on Shelley's part). Ianthe has a view of the receding earth. From a distance 'Tremendous Ocean' seems calm, then indistinguishable on the earth's 'vast and shadowy sphere':

> Earth's distant orb appeared
> The smallest light that twinkles in the heaven;
>> Whilst round the chariot's way
>> Innumerable systems rolled.   I, 250–3

All this puts man firmly in his place—but the system is also beautiful. As the chariot arrives at the temple of the Spirit of Nature the first part of the poem ends with an apostrophe to that Spirit. In this Shelley tries to reconcile the immensity of the universe with the microscopic life of earth. The 'lightest leaf/ That quivers to the passing breeze', and 'the meanest worm/That lurks in graves and fattens on the dead', and the 'interminable wilderness of worlds' are all filled with the 'eternal breath' of the Spirit of Nature.

Though man, therefore, has a place in the system it is not a privileged one—the Spirit of Nature inheres in everything that is inimicable to man (worms feeding on bodies), just as much as in man himself. Though he would not agree about how the universe was created, Shelley's position here is not very different from Pope's 'Whatever is, is right'. Existence is self-justifying.

The second part of the poem also deals with a theme recurrent in literature, the vanity of human wishes. The gorgeous dome of the Hall of Spells 'mocks all human grandeur'. Indeed, even a dwelling in a celestial palace cannot be the final reward of virtue since there, no less than on earth, it would be 'immured within the prison of itself'. This reflects Shelley's horror of self-sufficiency, the 'howl of self-interest' as he calls it in a letter to Elizabeth Hitchener. It is the first hint in his poetry of the search for an ideal otherness (derived at least partly from Plato on Love), which was for Shelley a necessary psychological condition. From the battlements the view of the apparently random but pre-determined movement of the universe, strangely both harmonious and eloquently silent, gives rise to explicit expression of Shelley's deterministic philosophy at this time:

> Countless and unending orbs
> In mazy motion intermingled,
> Yet still fulfilled immutably
> Eternal Nature's law.   II, 73–6

However, it is not merely the futility of human ambition that interests Shelley when he makes the fairy point out classic examples of it, such as the Pyramids. He is not even primarily interested in the humbling ravages of time, but in the exploitation involved in building such monuments. Nevertheless some architectural remains are preferable to others since they are melancholy reminders of a nobler time: 'Where Athens, Rome and Sparta stood/There is a moral desert now.' Greece is in subjection, and Rome the centre of the deceits of religion.

It might perhaps be objected here that Shelley makes a rather arbitrary and absolute distinction between civilisations he is in sympathy with and those he dislikes. More seriously, how can such judgments be allowed for in his deterministic view of nature? How can man's moral choices, and indeed history, be other than deterministic too? Such difficulties do not deter Shelley from inveighing against tyrants and priests. They and the corruption of wealth destroy what should be the unity of all men, and of man with the rest of nature. It is clear that Shelley *wants* to see man as part of a greater whole, and that he believes that the Spirit of Nature is equally inherent in the smallest individual particle of matter as in the solar systems. Admittedly this view was not new in literature. We could compare Pope's 'the green myriads of the peopled grass', or Marvell's grasshopper's-eye-view of Appleton House, with Shelley's:

> I tell thee that those viewless beings,
> Whose mansion is the smallest particle
> Of the impassive atmosphere
> Think, feel and live like man.   II, 231-4

The fascination with innumerable microscopic beings is the same. What is different is Shelley's obvious desire to teach a moral lesson, his suggestion that this apprehension should actually make a difference to the way men live.

Part 3 begins with Ianthe thanking Queen Mab for her perhaps rather oversimplified 'lesson not to be unlearned'. To reinforce the lesson, Queen Mab makes her look more closely at man. Down-trodden urban dwellers, soldiers, courtiers and kings pass in review, all alike miserable. The king is the 'wearer of a gilded-chain/That binds his soul to abjectness'.

It is not the weight of the cares of state complained of by Shakespeare's kings that oppresses Shelley's king; instead he prays for a drop of balm for his own 'withered soul'. This is a natural punishment. The king is despicable, but he is to some extent the victim of circumstances. Clearly it is very difficult for Shelley to decide on his attitude to the perpetrators of evil. He hates them but he shies away from punishment (the Christian idea of Hell was abhorrent to him). Shelley's great attempt to come to terms with this dilemma is *Prometheus Unbound*. In *Queen Mab* it is the evils of contemporary society that concern him. Miners' lives are merely protracted death. 'Many faint with toil/That few may know the cares and woes of sloth.' Clearly this is a terrible waste of human potential. It is unreasonable. When men learn to be reasonable, and therefore truly 'natural', the displays of wealth and power will seem what they really are, immature cravings. But there seems no logical reason, according to the law of the Spirit of Nature as propounded by Shelley so far, why the state of affairs should improve—tyrants are rarely opposed, and the outcome of the French Revolution, with the rise of Napoleon, was not encouraging. But such a situation is intolerable to Shelley. It is necessary to him to believe in the future, despite the 'record of crimes and misery'. So 'Tomorrow comes!' declares the fairy hopefully. Later in *Ode to the West Wind*, spring must follow winter. Responsibility for bringing about that future rests with the virtuous man who alone is free. He will neither bend to tyranny nor attempt to exercise command. Power 'pollutes'. Obedience 'makes slaves of men, and of the human frame/A mechanised automaton'. Man's obedience to a tyrant turns him into a machine, contrary to all 'Nature's suggestions'. Thus man sets himself against Nature's 'silent eloquence' of 'golden harvests' which declare that Love and Joy are the law of the universe. He makes himself an outcast.

A conflict arises here. Though Shelley is committed to the belief that man is capable of regeneration, that 'The pure diffusion' of the essence of the Spirit of Nature 'throbs alike in every human heart', it seems that man is outside the harmonious system. Can man, despite all the evidence to the contrary, ever hope to achieve equity? Judging by history, no. Judging by faith, yes. That Shelley's conclusion is essentially one of faith, based on an apprehension of beauty, is suggested by a change of verse form. The affirmation that man, too, unconsciously fulfils Nature's law is a song. It is both a vision and a prophecy, whose truth is attested, it seems, simply by its beauty. Shelley argues that the Spirit of Nature is a judge, outside man, whose power belittles all man's achievements, but also a spirit inhering in man himself as in all the other features of the universe. He also suggests, partly by the lyric metre, that there is a harmony in the universe, which is both naturally developing and consciously ordered, like art:

Spirit of Nature! thou
Life of interminable multitudes;
    Soul of those mighty spheres
Whose changeless paths through Heaven's deep silence lie;
    Soul of the smallest being,

    The dwelling of whose life
    Is one faint April sun-gleam;—
        Man, like these passive things,
Thy will unconsciously fulfilleth:
    Like theirs, his age of endless peace,
        Which time is fast maturing,
            Will swiftly, surely come;
And the unbounded frame, which thou pervadest,
            Will be without a flaw
Marring its perfect symmetry.   III, 226–40

The pattern has eternal qualities but depends upon process. The importance of localised and instantaneous beauty is suggested by the way time and space ideas are caught in the word 'dwelling'; but such moments are part of something much greater. Shelley puts together the notion of perfection and the notion of process. The frame pervaded by the Spirit of Nature is perfectly symmetrical and therefore defined; paradoxically it is also unbounded. By a similar poetic sleight of hand Shelley can equate both Necessity and Love with the Spirit of Nature. It is at once a scientific and moral principle.

The fourth section begins with an evocation of the beauty of the night, but its peace is shattered by a storm—in Arnold's phrase 'ignorant armies clash by night'. Ianthe is appalled by the horror left by conflict. At this time Shelley had not seen war. His descriptions lack the precision and particularisation of, for instance, Byron's noting of the 'all-white eye' of a corpse. But the idea is presented with a force calculated to shake the most confirmed optimism.

His repetition in the fourth section of 'Tomorrow comes!' casts an ironic light on the phrase used hopefully in Part 3. The morrow in this case brings slaughter, yet he refuses to accept that such things are inevitable. The fairy responds to Ianthe's unspoken doubt and horror by assuring her that war has specific causes which could be removed. To argue that it is caused by 'man's evil nature' is merely to excuse the perpetration of un-numbered crimes: 'Let the axe/Strike at the root, the poison tree will fall.' Conservative pessimism is for Shelley a falsification; man is redeemable. His proof of his assertion that 'A garden shall arise, in loveliness/Surpassing fabled Eden' is simply to take a look at Nature. It is plain from Nature's beauty that man is the odd creature out, the rest is harmony. Man's present state is not natural, he is merely conditioned by the corrupt institutions of society.

The child imitates his elders' aggressiveness in his games and is corrupted into thinking aggression heroism. Education serves merely to dim Reason. Though Shelley had a passion for learn-ing he deeply distrusted formal education. (In the letter to Godwin in January 1812 he claims that his own education was worse than useless: 'The knowledge which I have whatever it may be has been acquired by my unassisted efforts.') Moreover man's soul is 'bound/Ere it has life' by heredity, and the environment into which it is born. But even so, changes can be made in that en-vironment, and the soul can, presumably by an effort of will, resist pollution. Soul is for Shelley 'the only element'. Man can therefore choose to make the future better than the past.

It is however the evil of the present condition that preoccupies Shelley here. He returns to war, but now suggests its causes. These he believes to be the wretched motives of certain individ-uals or groups in society: statesmen, priests, lawyers and their parasites. Here Shelley's attitude is a bit more complicated than might at first appear. Once he has some identifiable targets he launches his attack on them with considerable gusto:

> the sinks and channels of worst vice,
> The refuse of society, the dregs
> Of all that is most vile   IV, 180–2

But he also gives a thought to the motives of those he is attacking. Their rage, he says, springs from 'hopelessness of good, and self-contempt'. Oppression, then, arises from the frustrations of pessimism; the oppressor destroys himself before he destroys others. The people Shelley scorns scorn themselves in that they deny their own potential for good. Indeed, this seems his principal objection to God, at least the God of priests and tyrants: 'A vengeful, pitiless and almighty fiend', invented to keep the people in subjection through fear of Hell and desire for Heaven. Thus Church and State are a gigantic conspiracy designed to give economic power to the few, who will be even further corrupted by the luxury and sensualism that affluence brings. The King is more wretched than his meanest subject:

> Are not thy days
> Days of unsatisfying listlessness?
> Dost thou not cry, ere night's long rack is o'er,
> 'When will the morning come?' IV, 247–50

No reasonable man, in Shelley's view, could possibly want to be a priest, conqueror or prince.

With a new generation new things are possible. This is presumably the implicit link between Part 4 and the rather arbitrary optimism introduced in Part 5. There is 'an imperishable change that renovates the world'. In a passage which is an anticipation of *Ode to the West Wind* Shelley sees the generations of man as dead leaves which, though they may smother all 'germs of promise' for many years, will eventually 'fertilise the land':

> Till from the breathing lawn a forest springs
> Of youth, integrity and loveliness,
> Like that which gave it life, to spring and die. V, 13–15

'Thus', declares Shelley, 'suicidal selfishness ... Is destined to decay.' Selfishness is religion's twin; it is the cause and effect of tyranny. Commercialism is its consequence, bringing 'pining famine and full-fed disease'. The workers, unable to escape the system, become 'scarce living pulleys of a dead machine/Mere wheels of work and articles of trade'. When Shelley says that 'The harmony and happiness of man/Yields to the wealth of nations', we see that the problems of his world are recognisably ours.

Shelley has the virtues and limitations of the well-heeled radical. It is easier for those who have had it than for those who have not to reject luxury, and to adopt a lofty moral tone about the 'grovelling hope of interest and gold'. The poor find it harder to believe that the rich are miserable. Certainly an old beggar Shelley had tried to engage in conversation the year before viewed him with some suspicion: 'You appear to be well-intentioned', he said, 'but I have no security of it while you live in such a house as that or wear such clothes as those.' Still, we should beware of accusing Shelley of hypocrisy.

Though in his youth he appears to have been preoccupied by his expectations, though his leisure for writing and reading depended upon a private income, he really did eschew luxury, from taste and conviction, as well as necessity. He was dismayed by the time servants spent tending mere objects, blacking grates for instance. 'To subject the labouring classes to unnecessary labour', he asserts in his notes to *Queen Mab*, 'is wantonly depriving them of any opportunity of intellectual improvement.' Like Gray he believes there are mute, inglorious Miltons, or Catos, or Newtons. 'Every heart contains perfection's germ.' Corrupt city life stifles it; crimes of violence are perpetrated not only to gain what the deprived lack but out of 'the deep stagnation of the soul'. Here again Shelley avoids a clichéd view. Just as he was not content to view hated tyrants merely as hated tyrants, so here he is not content to say 'Poverty breeds violence'. The causes are both subtler and deeper. This seems a remarkably up-to-date view of city violence in a money-based society.

Shelley was hardly alone in believing money is a root of evil. Avarice was traditionally a deadly sin. But it was money itself, rather than what it could buy, that was bothering Shelley's contemporaries. With increasing industrialisation, and the printing of paper money against which Cobbett for one waged a continuing campaign, more of the wealth of the nation was being gathered into the hands of a commercial *élite*. Shelley enlarges on this point in his notes to the poem. 'There is no real wealth but the labour of man.' Speculators boast themselves the promoters of the prosperity of the country because they employ the poor. This 'only aggravates whilst it palliates the countless diseases of society'. The factory hand is not working for essentials but to increase the goods which make up 'the daily and taunting prospect of . . . innumerable benefits assiduously exhibited before him'—and denied him.

Why should the workers most useful to the community be least valued and the purveyors of inessentials be so prosperous? 'The jeweller, the toyman, the actor gains fame and wealth by the exercise of his useless and ridiculous art; whilst the cultivator of the earth, he without whom society must cease to subsist, struggles through contempt and penury, and perishes by that famine which but for his unceasing exertions would annihilate the rest of mankind.' Economic power was passing from those with land, which involved certain inescapable responsibilities, to those with capital who did not necessarily have any contact with the workers who increased the value of that capital, or with the appalling conditions in which many of them worked. So there were inevitable connections between money and violence, between money and sensualism ('even love is sold'), and between money and war (waged by 'slave-soldiers').

From a negative assessment Shelley turns to a positive one. There is a nobler glory than the false military heroism little boys are taught to admire. This is the virtue of Reason uncorrupted by gold, fame or oppression:

> a life of resolute good
> Unalterable will, quenchless desire
> Of universal happiness.   V, 225–7

Though the pursuit of Reason is arduous, Shelley believes that it is possible and that the prospects were brighter than they had been: 'hoary-headed Selfishness has felt/Its death-blow'.

In spite of this assurance on the part of the fairy, Ianthe is still, at the beginning of the sixth section, understandably dispirited: 'Is there no hope in store?' The hope according to Queen

Mab lies in seeing things in the perspective of eternity. An ever-lasting soul can't be finally destroyed by doubts since it under-stands its situation. Even the 'perversest time' will produce 'some eminent in virtue'. Falsehood will destroy itself if the truth is sufficiently asserted, leaving the earth in harmony with the rest of the universe. However, Shelley is preoccupied with current evils, so Queen Mab returns once more to another onslaught on Religion, which, though repetitious, does contain Shelley's pithiest denunciation of it: that

> prolific fiend,
> Who peoplest earth with demons, Hell with men
> And heaven with slaves.   VI, 69-71

Then follows a flamboyant life history of Religion, from its infancy when natural objects were worshipped, to its tyrannical old age, when it is doomed and therefore desperate for violence and oppression. But just as in *Prometheus Unbound* and *Ode to the West Wind* spring must follow winter so here day must follow night. Religion's prideful glare 'fades before the sun/Of truth'. The image is useful to suggest an inevitable natural process, but it needs to be supplemented lest we should be driven to the gloomy conclusion that winter follows summer and night, day.

So Shelley reverts to machines and Necessity. 'A Spirit of activity and life' is the one constant in the 'storm of change, that ceaselessly/Rolls round the eternal universe.' With 'irresist-ible law' it apportions 'The place each spring of its machine shall fill'. Being a cog in the universal machine is the perfection of every atom. This is clearly at odds with his reluctance to view man as a 'mechanised automaton'. Here, however, Shelley adheres to Necessity as to a goddess even though it might seem that such a creed implies a sort of moral anarchy: 'the poison tree/And the fair oak are equal' to the Spirit of Necessity. In his notes he denies that this doctrine in the least diminishes 'our disapprobation of vice'. It is reasonable after all to kill a poisonous viper rather than be killed ourselves. Still it would be hard-hearted to do so in a situation where it was incapable of injuring us. For a Necessarian to feel hatred or contempt is inconsistent. He feels compassion for a criminal and has no desire to injure him. At least Necessity as God-substitute will destroy the 'almighty fiend' man has created. At least it admits multitudinous shapes of life, always pressing forward 'like hungry and unresting flames' round 'eternal columns'. Shelley's attraction towards an image of something lively and fluctuating near something eternal (like the simile for Ianthe's hair) suggests that he has a vision rather than a philosophy, and that he will have to dethrone Necessity.

The fairy now calls Ahasuerus to give a life history of God. The story of the Wandering Jew had much impressed Shelley. Ahasuerus combines 'the wisdom of old age' with 'youth's primeval dauntlessness'. So horrible, according to Ahasuerus, were God's cruelties and tyrannies that even Moses, the propounder of God's law of vengeance, is appalled. Shelley hates the *élitism* of both Judaism and Christianity. First Jehovah chooses a race who can sin with impunity, then sacrifices his son so that the elect may believe, damning the rest. Christianity is therefore a trick; while preaching peace, it promotes war. Christ's suffering on the Cross is mere make-believe, for challenging which Ahasuerus has been condemned to an eternity of wandering. Like Milton's Satan he prefers 'Hell's freedom to the servitude of Heaven'. Reason is, moreover, beginning to establish a reign of truth, through which its proponents can withstand the curses and torments of the tyrant. Though Ahasuerus here displays a degree of complacency not entirely dissimilar from Satan's pride—he is 'serene and self-enshrined'—his final analogy for himself shows him to be a forerunner of Prometheus. He is like a giant oak:

> peacefully and movelessly it braves
> The midnight conflict of the wintry storm,
> As in the sunlight's calm it spreads
> Its worn and withered arms on high
> To meet the quiet of a summer's noon.   VII, 262–6

The antagonist of Christianity displays some Christian virtues.

After Ahasuerus' departure the fairy turns from the past and present to the future. The vision of a harmonious life on earth is an inspiration to the human spirit. Through virtue it can arrive at the goal of universal peace. A paradisal age ensues; polar regions become habitable, deserts blossom, ocean-wastes are strewn with garden-isles, a child shares his morning meal with a 'green and golden basilisk/That comes to lick his feet'. As ferocious beasts become pacific, so man, with his greater potential for both good and ill, perceives the renovation; arctic savagery and tropic slavery are replaced by 'kindly passions'. This includes kindness to animals. Paradise is vegetarian. Meat-eating kindled 'putrid humours' and 'germs of misery'. The deposing of man from a pre-eminent position in creation, which shattered religious faith, is seen by Shelley as a way of hope:

> Man has lost
> His terrible prerogative, and stands
> An equal amidst equals: happiness
> And science dawn though late upon the earth. VII, 225–8

In this ecological heaven, reason and passion are no longer at odds.

The final part of the poem develops this point. In such an earthly paradise law is unnecessary—the only thing binding man is the bond of human sympathy. There is no need for 'selfish chastity' or for what Shelley saw as its inevitable corollary, prostitution. Free love brings about women's equality with men and the consequent liberation of both men and women. Churches and prisons, the citadels of oppression, would be given over to vegetation, birds and playing children. It is hardly surprising that one of a generation growing up just after the fall of the Bastille should include liberation from captivity and the destruction of prison walls in a paradisal vision. Emergence into light is the climax of Beethoven's *Fidelio*.

To realise this vision the human spirit needs steadfast courage. Already Shelley sees revolution as a gradual process like the processes of nature:

> Let virtue teach thee firmly to pursue
> The gradual path of an aspiring change. IX, 147–8

Birth and life and death all tend to perfect happiness. The dedication of the virtuous human spirit (such as Ianthe) must be two-fold: to attack the great abuses in society, 'tyranny and falsehood', that is, for Shelley, kingcraft and priestcraft, and to uproot 'the germs of misery from the human heart'. This is Shelley's own determination: as propagandist to defend the oppressed and to expose particular cases of injustice, and as a poet to change the hearts of men.

3

Alastor; The Hymn to Intellectual Beauty; Mont Blanc

Queen Mab dealt with the universe and society. Shelley's next main work, *Alastor*, deals with the self. It may seem surprising that the castigator of tyrants should have remained almost silent about the public events of the two intervening years. Apart from the short poem 'Feelings of a Republican on the fall of Bonaparte' there is no mention, even in the extant letters, of Napoleon's escape from Elba, for example, or the Battle of Waterloo. But enough had happened in his personal life to account for this: his estrangement from Harriet and consequent separation from his children, his elopement with Mary, his pressing financial problems, the death of Mary's first baby, his doctor's diagnosis (mistaken as it turned out) of fatal consumption. *Alastor*, written in the autumn of 1815, was the fruit of the first period of tranquillity after this turmoil. He had acquired an income of £1,000 a year, even if a large proportion of this was paid to Godwin and Harriet, and Mary was expecting another child. A boating holiday on the Thames as far as Lechlade, with a diet of mutton chops prescribed by Peacock, improved Shelley's health. His letters from this time mostly request books. One, the following spring, tells Southey that *Alastor* was 'the product of a few serene hours of the last beautiful autumn'.

The poem, writes Shelley, 'represents a youth of uncorrupted feelings and adventurous genius led forth by an imagination inflamed and purified through familiarity with all that is excellent and majestic, to the contemplation of the universe'. At first this large prospect satisfies him, but after a time he begins to long for and imagine a like-minded being. Failing to find this ideal he dies. Such a search is obviously doomed to failure, since self-love is involved in it. The search for the ideal otherness is a love affair with the self. Shelley recognises the narcissism but also the genuinely idealistic element. The poem, then, contains both self-glorification and self-criticism. Shelley, in the preface, emphasises the dangers of withdrawal from the world. He was himself tempted to this, partly because of the neglect or antagonism of others, and partly because of his innate fastidiousness. In spite of his political interests he very rarely read a newspaper. In spite of his concern for working people he had no desire to live among them—'It cost him much,' said Leigh Hunt, 'to reconcile himself to manners that were not refined.' Peacock reminds us that the word 'Alastor' means an evil genius—it is not the name of the Poet in the poem, but of the spirit of solitude as a spirit of evil. Shelley is taking stock of himself. Certainly Mary Shelley said that no poem is more characteristic of him. There are echoes of other poets, but the combinations are peculiarly his own.

Continuing one of the themes of *Queen Mab*, the poem opens with a fifty-line invocation to the brotherhood of earth, ocean and air of which man, too, is part. Some of the rhythms and constructions derive from Milton, as does the sense of the paradisal in nature. Some of the visual observations recall Wordsworth and Coleridge, though Shelley is more explicit about the brotherhood of man and nature. Wordsworth's Nature, though animated, is not personalised. The worst lines are pure Shelley —about spring's voluptuous pantings, or his own exploits among charnels and coffins. Where Shelley does imitate other poets he adds his own characteristic details. Lines 45–50 echo Wordsworth, but the combination of words relating to sound, texture and ideas in 'woven hymns/Of night and day' is Shelleyan. Indeed his preoccupation with textures and fabrics and with autumn winds and leaves runs through the poem. Leaves link the invocation and the opening with the Poet's untimely end. Shelley starts the poem after the death of his hero; the only pyramid built over his mouldering bones is one piled up by 'eddies of autumnal leaves'. This sets the tone for the poem, which combines vivid awareness of the beauty of nature with the frustration and disappointment involved in the search for the ideal, and the search for self.

The Poet of *Alastor* is a glamorised and mysterious figure, whose wild eyes, burning with soft fire, are particularly appealing to virgins. Desire for similar adulation was, one suspects, a motive for Shelley's penchant for finding young female disciples. His friends certainly noted his great attractiveness to women. However the *Alastor* Poet is not at all susceptible to the women, such as the Arab maiden (l. 129), who are actually there, presumably because even from his infancy he had been preoccupied with dreams and visions. His childhood was spent absorbing the influences of nature—quite Wordsworthian in fact. Sights and sounds were supplemented with fountains of secondhand knowledge, philosophy and fable. It is true that this information seems to have been absorbed rather than learnt, he 'felt and knew'. Presumably it was his intuitive powers that made him leave home, since Shelley at least does not bother to explain why the youth's home should suddenly be cold and 'alienated'. It is clear that, though Shelley has chosen to write of 'mind' and 'spirit', he is not interested in personal psychology, and though he is embarking on an allegorical travelogue he cares little about narrative.

The Poet's purpose in travelling is 'To seek strange truths in undiscovered lands', a line suggestive of romantic longing, perennially attractive to the reader—we think of Othello's accounts of his travels or Tennyson's Ulysses. The notion that the truth is difficult of access, and that it takes the adventurous spirit to search for it is appealing. But from another point of view the mission is suspect, since it implies that truth is where one is not, and that strangeness is one of its attributes, with the probable consequence that it ceases to be what one is looking for when one has found it. Arguably an unceasing and restless search for truth is a symptom of immaturity. Only two or three years before, both Southey and Godwin had been impressing on Shelley how young he was. It is not absolutely clear from *Alastor* whether Shelley is making a similar comment on his poet. 'Seeking strange truths in undiscovered lands' seems glamorous and heroic, but Shelley also says that deserted places 'lured' him. The mixture of poetic styles is not altogether happy; a sub-Miltonic Pandemonium untouched by devils' hands sorts oddly with a vegetarian idyll of antelope, squirrel and doves.

Shelley's touch is surer when the Poet leaves the wastes for a tour of famous ruins where 'dead men/Hang their mute thoughts on the mute walls'. The 'floating shades', suggestive of phantoms as well as shadows, give plausibility to the idea that the Poet is gaining an insight into the lives of past civilisations. The phrase Shelley actually uses for the thought process is harder to accept: meaning flashed on the Poet's vacant mind, purged, presumably, of the here and now, and 'he saw the thrilling secrets of the birth of time'. No reservations about the largeness of this vague assertion seem to be entertained by Shelley. Self-congratulation is not far distant.

The Arab maiden appears to have been introduced merely to admire the Poet. She brings him her own portion of food and her own matting to sleep on, she watches him sleeping, is awe-struck and never tells her love. The Poet neither takes advantage of her nor scorns her, he simply fails to notice her. The Arab maiden left behind, the Poet seems both vague (he wanders) and purposeful (he 'holds' his way 'in joy and exultation'). He is energetic enough to scale the peaks of Cashmir, but also poetically languid.

Characteristically Shelley becomes immediately more convincing when he leaves the physical and recounts the Poet's vision. He dreams of a veiled maiden sitting beside him. Unlike the Arab maiden, she speaks. Since her voice 'was like the voice of his own soul/Heard in the calm of thought', the Poet's subsequent search for her is clearly to some extent self-regarding. At the same time she is a separate entity, resembling the inspiration of nature. The music of her voice is like 'woven sounds of streams and breezes', as she discourses on his favourite exalted topics, philosophical, political and poetic. Her passionate behaviour is kindled by her pure mind, but she has obvious physical attractions. As with Ianthe, Shelley notices her 'branching

49

veins' as her hands sweep a harp. She seems demonic; her limbs are luminous, her veil is woven of wind and, as with most of Shelley's spiritual characters, her lips are parted. In a letter to Peacock four years later he notes with approval that Greek statues always have parted lips unless it is absolutely inappropriate—they seemed to him 'expressive of the exercise of the imagination and affections'. Both elements are presumably present here. The Poet's vision of the veiled and passionate maid fades as they ecstatically embrace—she 'folded his frame in her dissolving arms'.

The world as the Poet wakes seems cold, empty and garish. The rest of the poem deals with his itinerant attempt to fill that vacancy. Shelley makes it clear that it is misguided. The dream-embrace was treacherous, and the Poet 'overleaps the bounds' in his pursuit of a phantom. He is looking for death; rather as the gazer at his own reflection in a pool may be lured to drowning. Something of the sort later happens to the Poet when two eyes beckoning him on to a doom-laden voyage seem like his own eyes reflected in a pool. The eyes like the maid's music may be associated with stream and breezes, but the Poet is nonetheless quite literally self-regarding as he also is when he longs to deck his hair with yellow flowers which 'For ever gaze on their own drooping eyes' (presumably narcissi).

Shelley sees the Poet's passion for the veiled maiden as a sickness. It is a 'distempered dream' (l. 225), a poison (l. 229), it acts as a consumption (l. 252). The 'weary waste of hours' (l. 245) suggests both desert and decay; the landscape becomes progressively more desert too. The Poet is associated with autumnal death and finally covered with leaves. As his passion and travelling consume him he also seems more ethereal; at l. 259 he is like the Spirit of Wind, his feet not even disturbing the drifted snow; at l. 350 his frail form seems 'like an elemental god'. Desire for the ideal otherness soon becomes a death wish: 'a restless impulse' (l. 305) 'urged him to . . . meet lone Death on the drear ocean's waste'; the way to his love is via death (l. 369); he is led by 'love or dream, or god, or mightier Death' at l. 428; by l. 537 he almost seems a death-bringer himself—'from his steps / Bright flowers departed'. Nevertheless this impulse towards death is approved; it is (l. 492) 'the light within his soul'. And the Poet's death is decorated by Shelley; he is swan-like, increasingly calm and in tune with nature and obviously admired: 'The brave, the gentle and the beautiful/The child of grace and genius.' Like a fragile lute (l. 665) he has sensitivity and latent music, though he also shows concomitant weakness.

The search for the dream and the Poet's lingering death occupy 530 lines, the only events being changes of scenery. Their order seems arbitrary, though the final edge-of-the-world landscape is an appropriate locale for the Poet's peaceful and mystical end. Still Shelley manages to make much of this long journey interesting in spite of its disproportion. He varies the pace of the verse; the boat trip into the cavern, for example, moves excitingly to its vortical climax, and is then contrasted with a peaceful woodland scene. Some sections are given form by coherent imagery. In ll. 330-40, for instance, the images suggest that evening encloses the landscape in a tapestry. Shelley's love of boats and water and the trees of Windsor Forest, where he wrote the poem, accounts for some of the most memorable lines: the joints of the boat (l. 302), the wind 'blackening the waves' (l. 310), the falling spear grass (l. 411), the spires of windlestrae, the contrasts between various trees:

> The oak,
> Expanding its immense and knotty arms,
> Embraces the light beech. The pyramids
> Of the tall cedar overarching, frame
> Most solemn domes within, and far below.
> Like clouds suspended in an emerald sky,
> The ash and the acacia floating hang
> Tremulous and pale.   ll. 431-8

Boat and tree combine at l. 456 when Silence and Twilight 'sail' in the woods. Shelley notices moonlight effects precisely, too. A moon reflected in water is subtly different from its original—it looks 'vacantly/On the moon in heaven'; mist seems to absorb moonlight but excludes stars:

                                    Yellow mist
Filled the unbounded atmosphere, and drank
Wan moonlight even to fullness; not a star
Shone.   ll. 604–7

Here a characteristically expansive word 'unbounded' is justified
by its context. As the Poet is dying, precise visual description of
the two diminishing points of light of the crescent moon
disappearing below the horizon is linked with an equally precise aural effect; Shelley speaks of the 'alternate gasp' of the
Poet's 'faint respiration'. Shelley was interested in the physical
symptoms of illness—obsessively so at times, as when he convinced himself he had elephantiasis. But he is even more interested
in mental states. A number of the similes suggest that a visionary
or mental state, rather than a physical one, is the norm. At
l. 316 a boat is compared to someone floating in a silver vision.
It would be more usual to put it the other way round and
compare having a vision to being in a boat. At l. 472 human eyes
are like a human heart dreaming. Defining the physical in terms
of dream or vision suggests that Shelley, unlike most people,
felt that the spiritual world is more real than the physical.

  This tendency can also be seen in the *Hymn to Intellectual
Beauty* and *Mont Blanc*, composed on his 1816 visit to Switzerland. Indeed, without a narrative frame the tendency increases,
and some of the similes such as l. 45 of the *Hymn* or the mist and
cloud comparisons at l. 32 and l. 37 confuse rather than clarify.
Like *Alastor* both these poems represent a reaching out to an
ideal, Intellectual Beauty or, in *Mont Blanc*, the 'secret strength of
things'. Neither poem is as self-concerned as *Alastor*, but an
analogy is made in each between the mysterious workings of the
universe and the mysterious workings of man's mind. In the
Hymn each human being partakes of the unseen power though
the relation is shifting and obscure (stanza 1). Even those who
seem closest to the spirit of Beauty—the sage or the poet—
cannot explain the mysteries of life and pain and death. It is only
the occasional, momentary glimpse of Ideal Beauty, like half-
heard music or half-seen light, that 'gives grace and truth to life's
unquiet dream'. If this vision was constant, not transient, man

himself would be immortal (stanza 4). It is as though the perception of beauty is a sanction for belief in immortality. Without it the grave would be a 'dark reality'. Here the poet turns to his own experience:

> While yet a boy I sought for ghosts, and sped
>> Through many a listening chamber, cave and ruin,
>> And starlight wood, with fearful steps pursuing ...
> I shrieked, and clasped my hands in ecstacy!　　ll. 49–60

He 'sought' without success. Perception of the ideal beauty comes largely unbidden, and it cannot, it seems, be directly viewed. It was its 'shadow' which 'fell' on him as he was musing about life. The features of this stanza which seem most artificial, or 'poetic', are actually true. Shelley really did go ghost-hunting as a boy, and when he was excited his voice really did assume a very high-pitched tone. Stanza 6 links the poet's personal dedication to Intellectual Beauty with the world's need for that spirit's help in freeing it from 'dark slavery'. The personification of moments of time (they are actually going to be speaking characters in *Prometheus Unbound*) suggests an acute awareness of time's passage. The precipitance of youth, the desire for absolutes, for quick answers, indicated by ll. 49–52, give way to a more patient outlook in the last stanza:

> The day becomes more solemn and serene
>> When noon is past—there is a harmony
>> In autumn, and a lustre in its sky,
> Which through the summer is not heard or seen.　　ll. 73–6

The love of the ideal beauty exerts a more binding spell than poets can (l. 29). But it was Shelley's intention to help others perceive that beauty through his own 'frail spells'. They too would be bound to 'love all human kind'. Here the public vision of *Queen Mab* is linked to the private dream of *Alastor*.

'Rivers', said Shelley in a letter to Peacock a week before he wrote *Mont Blanc*, 'imitate mind, which wanders at will over pathless deserts and flows through nature's loveliest recesses, which are inaccessible to anything besides.' He is talking about a proposed boat trip, and is probably remembering the trip up the Thames whose meanderings are reflected in *Alastor*. But he has also been thinking about the Arve, originating in the snows and glaciers of Mont Blanc. Here is a river which can symbolise the impulses of thoughts, but also the enormous and mysterious energy of nature in which, in a small way, man participates. The day before he composed the poem he told Peacock that 'the immensity of these aerial summits excited, when they suddenly burst upon the sight, a sentiment of ecstatic wonder, not unallied to madness'. He describes an avalanche and the smoke of its path, and goes on to give a precise explanation of how the glaciers cause avalanches. The immediacy of this experience accounts for both the vividly recaptured sense of awe at the sight of river, ravine and sky, and also for an exclamatory tone and rather loose syntax which make the poem difficult to follow. Section 2, for instance, which contains 37 lines, has only one full-stop, and the proliferation of dashes and subordinate clauses in the whole poem suggests hasty composition and inadequate assimilation of the experience.

In the first section of the poem the scene before him provides Shelley with an analogy for the relationship between man's mind and the universe of which it forms a part. The external and the internal world are both mysterious. The 'everlasting universe of things' rolls like a river through the mind, and human thought (originating, Shelley vaguely explains, in 'secret springs') flows into it. Compared with the power of the apparently eternal river, bursting on rocks rather like the Alph in *Kubla Khan* (which by this time Shelley may have heard Byron recite), the human contribution to the universe is feeble:

> Power in likeness of the Arve comes down
> From the ice gulfs that gird his secret throne.

The mysteriousness of what the Arve symbolises is suggested by the shifting light and shade of a landscape, over which the shadows of clouds and sunbeams 'sail'—giving a sense of height and vista. The 'earthly rainbows' (l. 25) too are looked down on from a height. It is perhaps the vertiginous prospect of the 'Dizzy

Ravine' that makes Shelley so acutely conscious both of his own separateness as a single human being and of a passive readiness to be acted upon by the 'clear universe of things around'. His thoughts hover over the darkness of the ravine as he seeks a poetic image for it. That this darkness is metaphorical as well as actual is made clear by the third section which contains a number of questions to none of which Shelley can supply an answer. Has some 'omnipotence unfurled/The veil of life and death'? Is life really a dream? What can have been the origin of this stupendous landscape? The serene beauty of Mont Blanc can of itself inspire a sort of faith in nature, and seems almost a moral force.

The fourth section makes a contrast between the changeability of all living and dying things (with Shelley even dormant buds 'dream') and a remote serene universal Power. Life revolves around its inaccessible aloofness (II, 95–6) not unlike the flames revolving around marble in *Queen Mab* (II, 235–8). Of this the scene before him is an image. The glaciers may look like walls 'impregnable of beaming ice', like a solid, if dead city, but actually they are moving, a 'flood of ruin'. In the fifth section the snows, winds and lightning on the peak of Mont Blanc, unobserved but always active, become a symbol. They represent a 'secret' power which both gives the universe 'law' and 'governs thought'. Thus Shelley implies that natural laws and man's subconscious are somehow bound together.

In the poems of 1816, then, there is a turning inward to the self in *Alastor* with its decorative, semi-allegorical natural background. There is a new attitude to landscape in *Mont Blanc*, a poem where natural objects impress themselves on the poet, rather than being used by him as artistic props. Here Shelley attempts both to relate a personal ideal (as in *Alastor*) to an impersonal ideal (*Hymn to Intellectual Beauty*), and to reconcile the latter with what seems an impersonal power, having as much to do with destruction as with creation, with amoral energy as with private or political virtue. *The Revolt of Islam* (1817) attempts to incorporate all this material into a broader narrative framework.

4

The Revolt of Islam

The Revolt of Islam started life as *Laon and Cythna*, but when a few copies of this escaped from the press, the publisher got cold feet, fearing that the poem would alienate the public. He persuaded Shelley to make changes, the chief of which was to turn the lovers of the title from brother and sister into cousins. Incest crops up elsewhere in Shelley's work (as in other Romantic writers). In *Rosalind and Helen* incest between brother and sister is dealt with sympathetically; in *The Cenci* a father's incest with his daughter leads her to murder. In *The Revolt of Islam* it isn't important, and Shelley did not compromise his intellectual honesty by making the expedient change. What matters is that for Shelley similarity of interests and intellectual background was essential in a love relationship. Brothers and sisters share the same formative influences, and if Shelley is drawn to incest it is not so much because he wants to think of his sister as wife or mistress, as because he needs to think of his wife as having the same community of interest as a sister. In the Dedication to the poem Shelley addresses his own wife simply as 'dear Friend'.

Shelley made the changes readily because he wanted to influence people. In particular he wanted to fight despair. Men must believe in the possibility of human regeneration before the possibility can really exist. They must believe this in spite of the setbacks from Shelley's old enemies, priests and tyrants, and in spite of their recognition of the evil inside themselves. He puts this point clearly in his preface; he wants to arouse 'faith and hope in something good which neither violence nor misrepresentation nor prejudice can ever totally extinguish among mankind'. His intention is not to delineate an ideal system to replace corruption, but to make the reader more alive to the 'beauty of true virtue'. The poem will be a series of pictures: the results of oppression—civil war, famine—on the one hand; on the other the calm of mind of true patriotism and toleration.

Shelley believed his age needed a prophet of hope. Reactionary panic had spread like an epidemic after the French Revolution but was now, he thought, subsiding. How, after all, could any realist have expected a 'nation of men who had been dupes and slaves for centuries' to behave with exemplary moderation? If oppression didn't make the oppressed slavish or vengeful it wouldn't be the evil it is. Still it was hard for those who hoped the most from the original French rising, who had been most 'ardent and tender-hearted' to see it in this reasonable light. Many had been 'morally ruined' by it. Hence, he says 'gloom and misanthropy have become the characteristics of the age in which we live, the solace of a disappointment that unconsciously finds relief only in the wilful exaggeration of its own despair'. Now was the time for 'long-suffering and long-believing courage'.

Clearly Shelley's ideals are still the ideals of *Queen Mab*. But there are changes of emphasis. In the first place, though this new poem contains instances of improbable instantaneous conversions, greater stress is laid on the long-term nature of any campaign for human betterment. Reverses are given as much prominence as achievements. Secondly, more attention is given to individuals. In *Queen Mab* Ianthe is merely the worthy recipient of a vision; if she does anything it is only after the vision and poem are over. As we have seen, the intervening years had been ones of personal crisis and self-examination for Shelley, and in this poem individuals acting on their own, and individuals, united by love, acting together, have some impact on society at large. The two strands, political and private, are united by love. In *The Revolt of Islam*, says Shelley, 'Love is celebrated everywhere as the sole law which should govern the moral world.' Whereas *Queen Mab* is a philosophical poem in that it attempts to formulate a theory about the universe and man's place in it, *The Revolt of Islam* is primarily concerned with morality. It discusses the nature of evil, for instance, not to arrive at any coherent theory, but so that it may be conquered or its effects minimised.

At the start *The Revolt of Islam* is anchored to the time of its composition in two ways. Firstly, in the Dedication to Mary, Shelley speaks of her as one who has given him new inspiration. Secondly, the first person narrator, also inspired by a woman, is responding to the depressing aftermath of the French Revolution. However, it immediately becomes apparent that there is to be no further contact with actuality. The Poet's reaction to the failure of the 'last hope of trampled France' is to engage in rock climbing. Not, we gather, in order to precipitate himself from 'the peak of the aërial promontory' in despair, but rather to prove himself capable of positive action, perhaps to derive inspiration from nature and reawaken optimism. Here the narrator is given an opportunity to learn something about the nature of good and evil as a war between them is fought out before his very eyes, as he stands on his cliff overlooking a stormy sea. His attention becomes focused on one patch of sky, where he sees 'An Eagle and a Serpent wreathed in fight'. In the conflict Shelley concentrates on textures, on movement through space, and on volume. Eagle and snake are both unlike—'feather and scale'—and oddly alike: the bird's 'sinewy neck' (l. 241) resembles the reptile's 'lithe' one. The eagle's flight path seems almost as solid as the adamantine coils of the serpent round his neck (l. 229) which he eventually manages to shake off.

The conflict, though terrifying, is impressive as an expression of power and energy. As in *Queen Mab* the energy of nature seems neither good nor bad. It just *is*, and is therefore beautiful as well as appalling. We don't at this stage take sides in the struggle. As a kingly emblem of strength, with Biblical backing, eagles have attractions, but we are reluctant to applaud the predatory talons. Deceitful snakes, also with Biblical backing, need their heads bruising, but are also emblems of healing and wisdom. In *The Revolt of Islam* Shelley has it both ways. Later in the poem (IX, 3693) eagles are symbols of youthful strength and snakes (II, 701) of everything that is vile. Here however it eventually emerges that it is the eagle who represents evil and oppression and the snake who represents goodness.

The narrator was not the only witness of the struggle. Coming down to the sea shore, calm in the sunset, he sees a woman, 'beautiful as morning'. The simile is not merely decorative since this woman, like the veiled maiden of *Alastor*, brings inspiration and hope for the future. She too has a prophetic voice. She weeps for the wounded serpent, who, unlike the narrator, understands her strange and melodious language. It obeys her call and swims towards her to rest coiled in her embrace. She knows of the Poet's suffering and speaks to him in a voice that seems like a memory of a loved one. (Such memories are the subject of the 1821 lyric 'Music when soft voices die'.) She bids him dare to voyage with her, to learn how to combat despair. He follows, not because he really understands her words but to protect her from the serpent, who, though now at rest will surely attack and devour her. They embark in a magical gondola-like boat of moonstone (even boats in Shelley are like gauze or light), moving without sail or breeze through star-reflecting waves. The woman explains the origin of the conflict the narrator has witnessed. Two powers hold dominion over the world:

> Twin Genii, equal Gods—when life and thought
> Sprang forth, they burst the womb of inessential Nought.
>
> The earliest dweller of the world, alone,
>   Stood on the verge of chaos. Lo! afar
> O'er the wide wild abyss two meteors shone,
>   Sprung from the depth of its tempestuous jar:
>   A blood-red Comet and the Morning Star
> Mingling their beams in combat—as he stood,
>   All thoughts within his mind waged mutual war,
> In dreadful sympathy—when to the flood
> That fair Star fell, he turned and shed his brother's blood.
>
> I, 350–60

It seems then that good and evil both spring from the clash of creative energy. It is man, as observer and participant, who gives moral meaning to the warring energies. Man responds 'in dreadful sympathy' to what already exists in the world, but since the battle takes place only when the first witness arrives, it must also be, in some sense, a projection of his own inner conflicts. Shelley reverses traditional roles in his fall myth. The hurling down of his Lucifer (Morning Star) brings murder into the world; obviously evil has triumphed. The transformation in the next stanza of a beautiful, mild, starry shape into a 'dire snake' hated by man and beast is clearly the work of a fiend. No wonder man finds it difficult to recognise good when he sees it (I, 375–6). The real evil is a poison from which Fear, Hatred, Faith and Tyranny spread. That many people would not regard Faith as an evil though they would agree on the other three only goes to show how subtle and all-pervasive, in Shelley's eyes, the principle of evil is. He himself wanted to promote 'faith' in something good but distrusted dogmatic, institutionalised Faith.

So, the woman says, evil held sway in the early periods of the world's history but the Spirit of Good 'though in the likeness of a loathsome worm' turned. The people began to hope: first ancient Greece, then other civilisations have emerged from tyrannies. The cycle continues: the narrator has witnessed such a struggle and should not despair if tyranny seem again to assert itself. Such is the inspiration the woman gives and she now goes on to relate how the inspiration was born in her. Shelley's arrangement of story within story (and there are more to follow) may seem over-complicated, but it does suggest that he believes in a continuing rebirth of hope and goodness. A more serious drawback is that inspirers and inspired all sound remarkably like Shelley. We are back to the difficulty of *Alastor* that the man with a vision may seem, to some extent must be, self-absorbed. It was a central problem of Shelley's life as he struggled with 'the burr that will stick to one, the self'. Sure enough the mentor who inspired the woman was himself a poet, like Shelley 'a youth with hoary hair' who died young (as Shelley rightly believed he would) and like Shelley's Eton mentor, Dr. Lind, was able to teach pity through 'the record of crimes and misery'.

The woman, too, has a vision. She falls in love with an image of love, the Morning Star. Then in a dream she sees and loves a youth with the Morning Star on his forehead. (The 1821 lyric 'One word is too often profaned' deals with such love on a more human, personal level.) The relationship is as much familial as lover-like; she is his 'child' (l. 526). He leads her to a war-ravaged city, and teaches her to grieve but not despair. It is at this point (l. 541) that the narrator wakes up to the fact that the woman is not afraid of the snake. That is, in fact, almost the last we see of snake or woman in the poem. The boat approaches a *Kubla Khan*-like Temple, though, mixed up with Coleridgean ice and blossomy forests, are Shelleyan details: currents in water are 'marmoreal floods'; the carved moonstone porch roof casts flickering light on the statues (Shelley preferred sculpture to other visual arts), so that they almost come alive; the throne in the hall is like 'sculptured flame'. The diamond roof casts a prismatic veil, as later in *Adonais* life is seen as a dome of many-coloured glass; and Adonais becomes a star, as now the serpent does. Its two eyes merge into a single star crowning a shadowy form. Here as in *Prometheus Unbound* the ultimate reality is formless. All we know of it is that its light 'informs' dome, statues and listeners. The narrator is not the only new arrival. Also by translucent boat, as we learn in Canto XII, Laon and Cythna have come to the temple of the Spirit, but by a more difficult route—that of persecution and martyrdom. Laon's account of the events leading up to this forms the rest of the poem.

A résumé of the main plot is sufficiently ridiculous: Laon and Cythna, having grown up amid the beauties of nature and being students of history, are devoted to freedom and love (Canto II). When tyrants take over the country they are separated. Cythna is shipped off as a prisoner while Laon, having killed three men as he tried to protect her, is put in an unlikely pillar-dungeon. He is released by a hermit (Canto III) who nurses him through a seven years' madness. Then hearing of gathering liberation forces who have been inspired by a young girl whose virtue ensured her freedom (Cythna of course), Laon sets out for their camp (Canto IV). The Tyrant's troops savagely fall on the freedom-fighters while they sleep, but are eventually themselves surrounded. Laon prevents any vengeance-killing and the armies fraternise. The fallen Tyrant is left in his deserted palace with only a dancing child for company. The high priestess at the celebratory ceremony in honour of equality is none other than Cythna now known as Laone. A vegetarian feast follows (Canto V). Laon and Cythna are re-united (Canto VI), but foreign mercenaries called in by the deceitful Tyrant massacre the pacific vegetarians who have only pikes, the least reprehensible weapons, with which to defend themselves. Laon, the sole survivor, is rescued by Cythna on a gigantic horse. They flee together to a marble ruin. There they feed the horse and consummate their love. Later as Laon searches for food he sees the famine and pestilence left by war.

Cantos VII–IX consist of Cythna's account to Laon of her life while they were separated. The victim of the Tyrant's lust, and consequently intermittently mad, Cythna was taken to a half-submerged cave hideout by a dumb swimmer. Though she afterwards thought it was a delusion it seems that a daughter was born to her in the cave who was afterwards taken away through the waters by the same diver. Fortunately Cythna was kept alive by a friendly eagle which brought her food, but alas, no rope for escaping. It took an earthquake, rending the cavern, to set her free. Subsequently she was picked up by mariners who were converted to a love of liberty by her preaching and so set free their cargo of female prisoners. Arrived at the Tyrant's city, Cythna was mobbed by women fired by hopes of emancipation and by the inspiration of her humanity. The superstition-ridden and Tyrant-flattering priests were duly called out to curse her. Naturally the Tyrant was afraid of the desire for liberty and equality uniting a growing company of freedom-fighters, and the conflict that followed was the one in which Laon took part. Cythna is now serene in her love for Laon and for all mankind but she knows that the future is likely to be difficult and dangerous. Inspired by each other Laon and Cythna return to the tortured world.

Laon takes up the story again for Canto X. The Tyrant having leagued with foreign oppressors, feels, as he institutes a reign of terror, that he is a king indeed. Fear of Cythna's inspiration prompts an anti-creation, a six-day massacre leaving a terrible peace on the seventh day. Famine and plague create a waste land; in terror the people turn to religion. An Iberian priest calls for the burning of Laon and Cythna to appease the god, and a second massacre, of all infidels, ensues. Virtuous maidens calmly give themselves up to the slaughter. Laon leaves Cythna and, in a histrionic third person narrative describes how, disguised as a hermit, he appeared before the Tyrant appealing for love and joy: 'Fear not the future, weep not for the past.' The young who responded were killed by 'men of faith and law'. The supposed hermit promises to betray Laon to them if they will grant Cythna a safe conduct to America. This granted, he dramatically reveals himself as Laon. He jumps back to the first person as he prepares for martyrdom: 'I, Laon, led by mutes, ascend my bier/Of fire'. Once more Cythna arrives on horseback. The Tyrant breaks his oath and Cythna asks to be put on the pyre with Laon. As they die, the child (Cythna's daughter of course) who earlier danced for the Tyrant, swoons and reappears to them after death steering a pearl boat which conveys them on their death voyage to the Temple of the Spirit. Their arrival ends the poem.

Fortunately a preposterous narrative does not automatically disqualify a work from serious consideration—think of Wagner's *Ring*—and at least Shelley's heart is in the right place. There is indeed something rather operatic about *The Revolt of Islam* with its heroic conflicts, its arias about liberty and equality, its extended love interlude, not to mention the immolation of hero and heroine at the end. Doubtless analogies could also be made with painting—Laon on the splendid Tartar horse with its flaring nostrils and mane streaming in the thunderstorm would have made a fine romantic subject for Géricault, as would the heroic defence of a hill by the almost weaponless freedom-fighters falling before the enemies' swords. Of course, such pictures are not admired by everybody. The grandiose soon loses its appeal and there are many objections that can be made to *The Revolt of*

Islam. Whether these are outweighed by its virtues depends on the judgment and tolerance of the individual reader. Many may be repulsed by the hero's lack of modesty; Shelley needs the identification of a first person narrative to express his enthusiasm but this, uncomfortably, leaves Laon describing the triumphs of his own oratory. Worse still there is a discrepancy between what is claimed for Laon and what he actually achieves. It is amazing his name should have been remembered during the seven years he was mad; he may bring about a reconciliation between the armies (Canto V) but as the second attack begins he is ludicrously inadequate—'I leapt/On the gate's turret, and in rage and grief I wept.'

Two factors should be weighed against the self-glorification of Shelley's identification with Laon. In the first place it is necessary to think well of oneself before one can act nobly. This is a natural corollary of Shelley's hatred of retributive punishment, of priests who oppress the people with a load of sin and guilt, and it is the basis of his psychology for reform and hope for the future. Secondly Shelley's self-absorption is more than balanced by his veneration for the pure and noble in others. It is quite characteristic of Shelley that Cythna should be the more coherent figure in the poem and that the exposition of the philosophy of Love and Liberty should be put in her mouth rather than Laon's. Her effect on other people is more credible; her appeal, recounted by the hermit (Canto IV xviii), to the better nature of the guard ordered to torture her—'For thine own sake/I prithee spare me'—certainly ought to have had the inhibiting effect Shelley claims for it on anyone not utterly depraved by fear. Her plea for the emancipation of women and for a less authoritarian attitude to children is put clearly and concisely at Canto VIII, 3314–5:

> Woman as the bond-slave dwells
> Of man, a slave; and life is poisoned in its wells,

She sees that growing industrialism lures workers, hoping for profit, into a situation of slave-like dependency (Canto VIII, 3316–24). Her philosophy is consistently one of love and hope, opposed to morbid dwelling on the past, and to the paralysing self-contempt, which already in *Queen Mab* Shelley had seen as a great psychological evil:

> Reproach not thine own soul, but know thyself,
>   Nor hate another's crime, nor loathe thine own.
> It is the dark idolatry of self,
>   Which, when our thoughts and actions once are gone,
>   Demands that man should weep, and bleed and groan;
> O vacant expiation! Be at rest.—
>   The past is Death's, the future is thine own;
>   And love and joy can make the foulest breast
> A paradise of flowers, where peace might build her nest.
>
> VIII, 3388–96

At Canto IX Cythna links this with the idea of Necessity—evil will continue to be inextricably mixed up with good but Heroes and Poets and Sages can bequeath the inspiration of hope, love and liberty. Here Cythna shows her selflessness in that she doesn't look for posthumous fame for herself and Laon; it is enough for their ideals to live on. Though Shelley sometimes indulges in self-glorification, anonymous oblivion also has attractions for him. This is perhaps one reason for the recurrence of the autumn leaves image. As Cythna sings her hymn to Equality, her voice:

> was as a mountain-stream which sweeps
>   The withered leaves of Autumn to the lake,
> And in some deep and narrow bay then sleeps
>   In the shadow of the shores; as dead leaves wake
>   Under the wave, in flowers and herbs which make
> Those green depths beautiful when skies are blue . . .
>
> V, 2281–6

In *Queen Mab* we saw subterranean life working, here Shelley adds underwater life. Both these find expression again in the *Ode to the West Wind*. An even clearer hint of that poem appears at Canto IX, 3649–57:

> The blasts of Autumn drive the winged seeds
>   Over the earth, —next come the snows, and rain,

> And frosts, and storms, which dreary Winter leads
>> Out of his Scythian cave, a savage train;
> Behold! Spring sweeps over the world again,
> Shedding soft dews from her ethereal wings;
>> Flowers on the mountains, fruits over the plain,
> And music on the waves and woods she flings,
> And love on all that lives, and calm on lifeless things.

Shelley's tendency to over-simplification and to hysterical generalisation is apparent in *Queen Mab*. It mars *The Revolt of Islam* too. His handling of his cast of thousands is often ludicrous; armies appear on the scene only to be eliminated with lightning rapidity; improbable feats are accomplished in the twinkling of an eye. The mind boggles, for instance, at the co-operative overnight construction of an enormous pyramidal marble altar complete with 'rare' sculptures in Canto V. Like Milton's Pandaemonium it rises to the sound of aerial music, but unlike Milton Shelley neglects to provide an architect. It is created in one night by 'the devotion of millions' with, it seems, but one architectural as well as political ideal and with improbable engineering skill. There are, however, occasions when Shelley provides a poetic context which makes what would in sober reality be ridiculous seem less so. Cythna looks supernatural as she makes her horseback rescue of Laon mainly because of her white robe gleaming in the twilight. Laon's hysteria (Canto III, 1270 onwards) is real hysteria leading into madness. When Laon searching for food meets Pestilence we find he is not meeting a personification but a woman driven mad by grief and hunger. Here there is also more of a sense of dramatic structure than might at first appear. The mad woman drags Laon to a hut where she has laid out three piles of loaves for a 'feast'. Horrifically, the guests, placed seated in a circle, are stiff, dead babies. This is both parody and logical sequence of the bloody 'feast' of the Tyrant's troops in Canto VI, itself a sequel to the vegetarian feast of celebration in Canto V.

This brings us to the two qualities of Shelley's writing in *The Revolt of Islam* for which, it seems to me, much may be forgiven him. He may often be careless of the reader—how many are likely to know what a 'hupaithric' temple is?—but he has the courage to be morally consistent even when there are unfortunate consequences; and he is capable of creating striking pictures to express his ideal. For instance, though we may feel that Laon was naïve not to keep the ex-tyrant under more restraint, he is consistent in his adherence to the ideal of forgiveness. It had been his call to the freedom-fighters to refrain from vengeance that brought about the spontaneous peace between the armies, leading to the Tyrant's deposition. In any case Shelley disapproved of letting the end justify the means—'I never will do evil that good may come' he once wrote to Elizabeth Hitchener. Shelley is also consistent in presenting love rather than duty as the source of virtue. A combination of strength and mildness marks out the good characters, male and female alike. Individuals and nations are 'made free by love', or as an admirer of Shelley, George Bernard Shaw, said 'Guarantee a man's goodness and his liberty will take care of itself'. Love is the basis of justice:

> What call ye *justice*? Is there one who ne'er
>   In secret thought has wished another's ill?—
> Are ye all pure? Let those stand forth who hear,
>   And tremble not. Shall they insult and kill,
>   If such they be? their mild eyes can they fill
> With the false anger of the hypocrite?
>   Alas, such were not pure, —and the chastened will
> Of virtue sees that justice is the light
> Of love, and not revenge, and terror and despite.

> V, 2017–25

So a possibility of regeneration is extended to the fallen tyrant; he is fed and is granted an image of tenderness and grace in the child who dances to cheer his desolation. The child's spontaneous kindness is one striking picture of ideal humanity in the poem. Similarly—and this is basic to Shelley's thinking—it is not, as some superstitious people think, any divinity in Cythna that is the source of her inspiration to others, it is her humanity: 'my human words', she says, 'found sympathy/In human hearts'. Vegetarianism, too, is based on an extension of the feeling of comradeship for one's fellow beings. In Canto X Laon recalls

67

'friendly sounds from many a tongue which was not human', and Cythna had cause to be grateful to her eagle.

Just as love not law should be the basis of public life so it should govern private life. 'Lawless love' (Canto V, 2231) does not mean illicit sex but the love of free and equal men and women. Indeed the presentation of both the spirituality and the physicality of the love between Laon and Cythna is Shelley's most remarkable achievement in the poem. The 'wide and wild oblivion of tumult and of tenderness' is introduced by one of Shelley's favourite boat images:

> We know not where we go, or what sweet dream
>   May pilot us through caverns strange and fair
> Of far and pathless passion, while the stream
>   Of life, our bark doth in its whirlpools bear,
>   Spreading swift wings as sails to the dim air;
> Nor should we seek to know, so the devotion
>   Of love and gentle thoughts be heard still there
> Louder and louder from the utmost Ocean
> Of universal life, attuning its commotion.   VI, 2587–95

This sense of being a part of an on-going life process and an acceptance of its mystery also infuses Cythna's conversation with Laon at the end of Canto IX. She is conscious of being part of its obscure stream: 'All that we are or know, is darkly driven/ Towards one gulf.' Both *Prometheus Unbound* and *Adonais* are, amongst other things, attempts to come to some terms with this ultimate obscurity. In *The Revolt of Islam*, in spite of all its un-realistic preposterousness, it is humanness that counts. Paradise for Laon is not the contemplation of the Heavens but the smile of Cythna.

5

1818-19: 'All my saddest poems . . .' *Julian and Maddalo*; *Stanzas written among the Euganean Hills*; *Lines written in Dejection, near Naples*

After *The Revolt of Islam* came another period in Shelley's poetic life of at least partial withdrawal from public concerns to private preoccupations. True, he made a start on *Prometheus Unbound*, but the poems discussed in this chapter reflect the difficulties and distresses of his first year in Italy. After a stop in Milan the Shelleys moved to Pisa, then to Leghorn, settling at the end of May 1818 at the Bagni di Lucca. In spite of landscape and climate, Italy had painful aspects. The streets of Pisa and Rome were cleaned by chained convicts; later the first thing Shelley saw in Naples was an assassination. Though the Shelleys made friends with the Gisbornes (who knew the Godwins) they were rather lonely. Besides there were difficult negotiations with Byron to allow Claire to see Allegra who was with him in Venice. Shelley had to mediate between them. The attempt to see Allegra resulted, indirectly, in the death of Shelley's own daughter Clara. Shelley travelled to Venice from Pisa with Claire and later asked Mary to join him. So the baby was taken on an awkward and protracted journey at a bad time of year. As Mary's journal tersely puts it: 'On Thursday (24 September) I go to Padua with Clara; meet Shelley there. We go to Venice with my poor Clara who dies the moment we get there.' Shelley's health, too, was poor at this depressing time so after a stay in a villa lent by Byron at Este they moved south to Naples for the winter, and to Rome the following spring.

One of the mysteries of Shelley's life belongs to this period. In Naples Shelley registered the birth of a daughter Elena Adelaide Shelley. It seems unlikely that he was her father. Since Oxford days he had wanted to adopt a daughter, and at Marlow had temporarily taken charge of a village girl. In 1821 two servants, dismissed by the Shelleys, tried to blackmail them, claiming that the Neapolitan child was Claire's and that Shelley was the father. Mary as well as Claire and Shelley emphatically denied this and it is inconceivable that Mary should have been ignorant of the birth if, as the servants claimed, it had taken place in her house. This child died in June 1820 and never actually lived with the Shelleys.

The sadness of this year finds its way into his poems but scarcely into his letters, which are concerned with new impressions: Italian landscape and cities, Italian painting and literature, Plato and classical sculpture. He takes 'great delight in watching the changes of the atmosphere', and the pale summer lightning: 'no doubt Providence has contrived these things that when the fire-flies go out the low flying owl may see her way home'. The waters in the Bay of Naples are 'forever changing, yet forever the same'. Beneath the waters he peers at 'hollow caverns, clothed with the glaucous sea-moss and the leaves and branches of those delicate weeds that pave the unequal bottom of the water'. In Venice he enthusiastically compares gondolas to 'moths of which a coffin might have been the chrysalis'. Rome strikes him as 'a city of the dead or rather of those who cannot die', the present inhabitants as 'puny generations' compared to the glorious classical past.

More recent artistic monuments fail to gain his approval. Michelangelo's Day of Judgment in the Sistine Chapel is a 'kind of Titus Andronicus in painting'. God seems to be 'eagerly enjoying the final scene of the eternal tragedy'; Christ is a figure of 'commonplace resentment'. St. Peter's exhibits 'littleness on a large scale', while the ancient Pantheon, though only a quarter the size, is 'the visible image of the universe; in the perfection of its proportions, as when you regard the unmeasured dome of Heaven, the idea of magnitude is swallowed up and lost'. After seeing Pompeii he understands 'why the Greeks were such great Poets', and above all can account 'for the harmony, the unity, the perfection, the uniform excellence of all their works of art. They lived in a perpetual communion with external nature and nourished themselves upon the spirit of its forms. Their theatres were all open to the mountains and the sky. Their columns that ideal type of a sacred forest with its roof of interwoven tracery admitted the light and wind, the odour and the freshness of the country penetrated the cities'.

Shelley's judgments of the visual arts and of literature are governed by two principles—the search for ideal unity and the search for moral usefulness. Though so much of his own work is obviously flawed and lacking in structural unity, the search for an ideal behind the outward forms of nature and shifting human life pervades it. 'You know', he wrote to Peacock at this period, 'I always seek in what I see the manifestation of something beyond the present and tangible object.' This remark is prompted by his examination of Tasso's handwriting which he sees as 'the symbol of an intense and earnest mind exceeding at times its own depth'. In the same letter a lament that paintings are evanescent leads him to a consideration of the relationship between art and morality foreshadowing the *Defence of Poetry* of 1821 (see Chapter 11): 'The material part indeed of these works must perish, but they survive in the mind of man, and the remembrances connected with them are transmitted from generation to generation. The poet embodies them in his creation, the systems of philosophers are modelled to gentleness by their contemplation ... men become better and wiser.' It is on moral grounds that he thinks Michelangelo and Ariosto overrated; both seem to celebrate impulses of revenge. Ariosto is lacking in 'The gentle seriousness, the delicate sensibility, the calm and sustained energy without which true greatness cannot be ... He constantly vindicates and embellishes revenge in its grossest form, the most deadly superstition that ever infested the world.' In another letter to Peacock two months later Shelley says 'I consider Poetry very subordinate to moral and political science and if I were well I should certainly aspire to the latter'.

But Shelley was not well and the poems of the period reveal that he was not happy. To his publisher he referred to them as all his 'saddest poems raked up into one heap'. Mary, perhaps feeling that Clara need not have died, was intensely depressed and withdrawn. Shelley hid his more personal poems from her and when she collected them after his death she looked back 'with unspeakable regret and gnawing remorse . . . fancying that had one been more alive to the nature of his feelings, and more attentive to soothe them, such would not have existed'.

Of two short lyrics revealing Shelley's depression, 'The Past' may well reflect estrangement from Mary and a sense of her present inability to look to the future:

> Wilt thou forget the happy hours
> Which we buried in Love's sweet bowers,
> Heaping over their corpses cold
> Blossoms and leaves, instead of mould?
> Blossoms which were the joys that fell,
> And leaves, the hopes that yet remain. ll. 1–6

'That joy, once lost, is pain' (l. 12) is a feeling that Shelley had already poignantly expressed in a fragment written in 1816 about home:

> Dear home, thou scene of earliest hopes and joys
> The least of which wronged Memory ever makes
> Bitterer than all thine unremembered tears.

Increasingly it becomes the characteristic note of his shorter lyrics, running counter to his political and philosophical optimism. The slightly self-congratulatory idea that he was destined to a brief but intense life sobers into the feeling expressed in 'On a faded violet' (1818) that he had better not exist:

> The odour from the flower is gone
>   Which like thy kisses breathed on me;
> The colour from the flower is flown
>   Which glowed of thee and only thee!

Shelley at twenty-seven

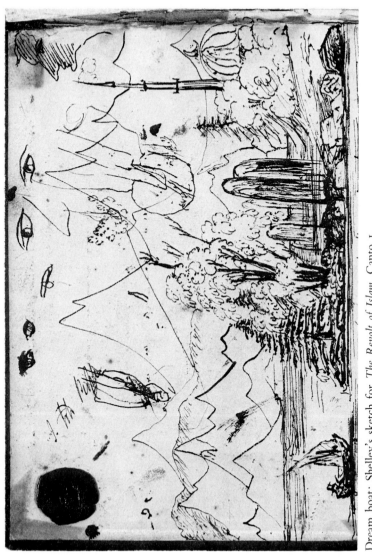

Dream boat: Shelley's sketch for *The Revolt of Islam*, Canto I.

Paddle boats: a page from Shelley's draft of *The Mask of Anarchy*.

Mary Shelley: 'Child of love and light'.

A shrivelled, lifeless, vacant form,
 It lies on my abandoned breast,
And mocks the heart which yet is warm
 With cold and silent rest.

I weep,—my tears revive it not!
 I sigh,—it breathes no more on me;
Its mute and uncomplaining lot
 Is such as mine should be.

Perhaps remorse for Harriet is suggested by Stanza 2, a temporary bleakness in his relationship with Mary by Stanza 1. Possibly
both contribute to the rather puzzling figure of the madman in
Julian and Maddalo.

Shelley declares in his preface to *Julian and Maddalo* that he can
give no information about the maniac, but that he seems to have
been disappointed in love. Julian is Shelley himself, 'passionately
attached ... susceptible'. Maddalo (Byron) takes a wicked
delight in drawing out his taunts against religion, and is, according to Shelley, 'proud'. Shelley admired Byron's genius (as the
1821 sonnet to him shows) but he believed that he misused his
abilities, that 'his sense of the nothingness of life prevented him
from doing all the good to his fellow men that he might'. The
story of the poem is simple: Julian and Maddalo ride along the
beach near Venice, the evening landscape produces friendly
philosophical conversation. From a distance they see and hear
the bell of an island lunatic asylum. Next day, at Maddalo's
suggestion, they visit one of the inmates, who once held the same
philosophical views as Julian. Julian, feeling close sympathy for
the madman, would have liked to befriend him, but is called
away from Venice by business. Many years later Maddalo's
daughter (Allegra) tells Julian that the madman is dead.

The poem reflects two sides of Shelley. The first part shows all
the qualities that made him at ease in company: his acute
observation, his affability, his capacity for friendship—with an
aristocratic intellectual or with a child. The second part reveals
his sense of isolation, of failure, of being injured, of dedication to
tenderness. His descriptions of landscape and skyscape show a

73

new precision, sharpened by his study of Italian scenes and paintings. For the first time he uses couplets flexibly, easily combining description, aphorism, casual comment, and philosophical discussion. The first part of the poem displays a new ability to assess and evaluate his emotions coolly and with some complexity, both in relation to landscape and in his readiness to present conflicting views. The opening description of the 'bare strand/Of hillocks, heaped from ever-shifting sand/Matted with thistles and amphibious weeds' is allowed to speak for itself:

> an uninhabited sea-side,
> Which the lone fisher, when his nets are dried,
> Abandons; and no other object breaks
> The waste, but one dwarf tree and some few stakes
> Broken and unrepaired, and the tide makes
> A narrow space of level sand thereon,
> Where 'twas our wont to ride when day went down.
>
> ll. 7–13

When Shelley does comment on it he combines direct statement of personal preference with a slightly wry appeal to common experience:

> I love all waste
> And solitary places; where we taste
> The pleasure of believing what we see
> Is boundless as we wish our souls to be.   ll. 14–17

The style is more economical. His comparison, in a letter to Peacock the same autumn, of clouds 'struck by the clear north wind' to 'curtains of the finest gauze removed one by one' is condensed to:

> the blue heavens were bare
> Stripped to their depths by the awakening north.   ll. 23–4

Similar economy appears in the description of the calm of the Venetian waters:

> the flood
> Which lay between the city and the shore
> Paved with the image of the sky.   ll. 65–7

Or of the belfry on the island they later pass in Maddalo's gondola:

> on the top an open tower, where hung
> A bell, which in the radiance swayed and swung. ll. 102–3

Sunset predictably provokes more elaborate expression, though even here Shelley's favourite fabric imagery is understated—we only know he is comparing the sky to a tent by the word 'rent' in l. 74.

The conversation during and after the ride combines some intensity of speculation with a sense of an easy social occasion. We see this in the casual comment on a commonly felt change of mood from exhilaration at the start of an expedition to reflection as one turns home, 'which always makes the spirit tame'. The conversation is governed by the atmosphere of the surroundings and the shifting moods of the participants. After joking reminiscence on the outward ride they talk of 'all that vain men imagine or believe/Or hope can paint or suffering may achieve', Julian trying to counteract Maddalo's darker view. Julian's indignation when Maddalo tells him that the bell is calling lunatics to vespers provokes a joking reference to the innocuous-looking Shelley's dangerous opinions—he is 'a perilous infidel/A wolf for the meek lambs'. Shelley captures Byron's abrupt shifts of mood (so apparent in *Don Juan* especially) as he compares the human soul to the silhouetted bell. The expedition ends as the light fades.

A sense of fidelity to remembered experience is conveyed in some details of the second paragraph. Shelley doesn't glamorise the weather, it was 'rainy, cold and dim'. His description of his renewal of friendship with Allegra while he waits for Maddalo—'We sate there, rolling billiard balls about'—captures the memorability of desultory experiences. Shelley doesn't need to tell us that billiard balls would be the toys to hand in the Count's house or that the two are sitting companionably together on the floor. When Maddalo appears the child becomes an object of comparison in adult conversation, as Julian contrasts her freedom and happiness with Maddalo's 'sick thoughts' of the preceding evening. He takes up the argument again, asserting man's essential freedom: 'We might be otherwise—we might be all/We dream of'. This is an opinion Shelley had expressed in a letter to Mary that September: 'There is nothing which the human mind can conceive, which it may not execute; Shakespeare was only a human being.' As in *The Revolt of Islam* we see Shelley's idea of the supreme value of humanness. 'You talk Utopia', rejoins Maddalo. That his own view is not simple-minded Julian shows by stressing that strength may appear through suffering as well as action:

> we know
> That we have power over ourselves to do
> And suffer—what we know not till we try.   ll. 184-6

It is religion, he implies, that makes men acquiesce in the *status quo*. Maddalo cannot agree with Julian's optimism; while admitting that such a philosophical system might be 'refutation-tight/As far as words go' he appeals to experience for refutation of it. He therefore proposes the visit to a man who used to argue like Julian, but is now an inmate of the asylum.

Most of the rest of the poem is concerned with the story of the madman and his melancholy ravings. Though some critics have seen this section as the residue of an attempt by Shelley at a tragedy dealing with the madness of Tasso (he wrote movingly in a letter about visiting Tasso's prison), or a version of a story going the rounds in Venice at the time, it is tempting to see something of Shelley himself in it. The madman has been deserted by one he loved. Shelley must have thought about deserted Harriet. Perhaps he felt that Mary was estranged from him and that therefore, like the madman, he could not speak his own grief, but had to wear a 'mask of falsehood even to those/Who are most dear'. Similar desire for pity (339-40) crops up later in the lyric 'One word is too often profaned', when Shelley is not obviously adopting a persona. Certainly in real life he looked to women for comfort and pity as well as admiration—Mrs. Boinville and her daughter for instance. The madman's dedication as a boy to justice and love (381) recalls Shelley's own, referred to in Stanza 4 of *The Revolt of Islam*'s Dedication. And the madman's hypersensitivity—'Me—who am as a nerve o'er which do creep/The else unfelt oppressions of this earth'—has too much in common with the hero of *Alastor* not to be connected with Shelley himself.

To Julian, the lunatic's disjointed speech seems poetic. But it is rather a relief to be returned to Maddalo's urbane, aphoristic style:

> Most wretched men
> Are cradled into poetry by wrong,
> They learn in suffering what they teach in song.   ll. 544–6

The good, particularly the poetic good, that can emerge from suffering is a recurrent theme in *Alastor*, *Prometheus Unbound* and the ode *To a Skylark*.

Though the depressed side of Shelley may, like the madman, have indulged the feeling that all that remained for him was to forgive and die—and a clear death wish appears in *Stanzas Written in Dejection, near Naples*—the forward looking part of him provides a coda in which he imagines Allegra grown up 'like one of Shakespeare's women'. She welcomes Julian and talks of her father. The prophetic postscript is sadly ironic. Allegra died when she was five. Byron was not, as she tells Julian, travelling in Armenia, but buried at Missolonghi; and Shelley was long since drowned.

Shelley composed the *Lines written among the Euganean Hills* in October 1818 at the villa lent him by Byron at Este near Venice. It stood on the brow of a foothill of the Alps. The view from the garden over the plain of Lombardy, bounded to the west by the distant Apennines and with the horizon to the east 'lost in misty distance', forms the basis of the poem. The sea-like plain 'islanded' by cities is an analogy for the drear and lonely voyage towards death, only occasionally alleviated by brief sojourns on green flowering islands. From his hill-top Shelley surveys the real and metaphorical landscape. Of these the actual is infinitely more impressive. The 'solid darkness' closing round the vessel's track (7) is the one sharp detail in the allegory, itself quickly engulfed by self-pity and Shelley's obsession, here irrelevant, with tyrants (45–60). Two insights into Shelley's state of mind are incidentally revealed in the first part: his realisation of his double attitude to death, 'longing with divided will' for the distant shore and 'haven of the grave;' and a sense of the irrevocability of the past (35–6). Shelley's touch becomes much surer when he turns to the actual landscape. The rooks' blackness is hoary in the morning mist, then gilded by the early sun. He is fascinated by the effect of sun and mist on the sea, canals and buildings of Venice in the distance. In the precise observation and assured evocation of light on water and towers in ll. 90–110 he anticipates Turner who painted his first water-colours of Venice the following year. The magical appearance of the towers 'quivering through aërial gold' belies, he says, the present degradation of Venice under Austrian rule.

As the morning light shifts from Venice Shelley's attention turns to Padua set amongst the harvests of the plain where 'milk-white oxen slow/With the purple vintage strain'. Its subjugation has extinguished the lamp of learning, and Shelley fears for the future since a 'despot's rage' sows slaves' revenge. Once again as Shelley moves (285) from his public concern to the landscape spread out before him his verse becomes more assured, the seven-syllabled lines less obtrusive. The panorama—'curved horizon', 'plains', 'the olive-sandalled Apennine', the snows of the Alps—and the foreground details of flowers and frosted autumn leaves, combine into a harmony in which he can share. As his soul and nature are 'interpenetrated', 'the frail bark of this lone being' (330) is briefly havened, before he has to embark again on the 'sea of Life and Agony'. Shelley's temporary resting encourages him to think that a paradisal retreat might be found in which he could be secure and guiltless with those he loves, and in which this private love could expand to include regenerate multitudes 'and the earth grow young again'.

In *Lines written among the Euganean Hills*, the harmony of landscape absorbs Shelley, but in *Stanzas written in Dejection, near Naples* he feels excluded from it because he is one 'whom men love not'. He needs someone else to share in his emotion before he can feel, as opposed to see, the beauty around him. His state of mind is not unlike that of Coleridge in *Dejection, an Ode*, but whereas Coleridge's attempts to impose a theory on his experience, or lack of it, lead him eventually to an apostrophe to joy, Shelley's poem is subdued to one mood. Shelley makes music out of despair.

> Alas! I have nor hope nor health,
>   Nor peace within nor calm around,
> Nor that content surpassing wealth
>   The sage in meditation found,
>   And walked with inward glory crowned—
> Nor fame, nor power, nor love nor leisure.
>   Others I see whom these surround—
> Smiling they live, and call life pleasure;—
> To me that cup has been dealt in another measure.
>
> Yet now despair itself is mild,
>   Even as the winds and waters are;
> I could lie down like a tired child,
>   And weep away the life of care
>   Which I have borne and yet must bear,
> Till death like sleep might steal on me,
>   And I might feel in the warm air
> My cheek grow cold, and hear the sea
> Breathe o'er my dying brain its last monotony.   ll. 19–36

Here is one of the unconscious previsions of the 'sublime fitness' of his end. Shelley's fascination for boats and water seems to represent the opposed impulses, present in all of us, but felt especially keenly by him, towards life and death. Boats suggest the on-goingness of life, water the oblivion of death. As we shall see when we come to *Adonais*, ultimately for Shelley the two are the same. In his poems his boats tend to drift, to be carried on the river of life or to have supernatural pilots. His oceans may bring merciful escape from the self, but they also nourish life, as they do in lines 360–1 of *Lines written among the Euganean Hills*, or in the *Ode to the West Wind*. He was fascinated, as we have seen, by the vegetation under the water of the Bay of Naples. This seems to parallel in his poetic thought a paradox of his temperament. He had an extraordinary purposefulness—'I go on until I am stopped and I never am stopped'—and Trelawny remarked of him that 'when attacked he neither fled nor stood at bay, nor altered his course but calmly went on with heart and mind intent on elevating his species'.

But Trelawny also mentions Shelley's curious passivity when he tried to teach him to swim: 'Shelley loved everything better than himself. Self-preservation is, they say, the first law of nature, with him it was the last ... He doffed his jacket and trousers, kicked off his shoes and socks and plunged in, and there he lay stretched out on the bottom like a conger eel, not making the least effort or struggle to save himself. He would have been drowned if I had not instantly fished him out. When he recovered his breath he said: "I always find the bottom of the well, and they say Truth lies there. In another minute I should have found it and you would have found an empty shell. It is an easy way of getting rid of the body".' He had been quietly determined to sink to the bottom rather than let Byron risk his life saving him when their boat was caught in a squall on Lake Geneva in 1817. When, in a later boating accident near Pisa, he was told to be 'calm and quiet' his answer was 'All right, never more comfortable in my life; do what you will with me'. Unlike Williams, Shelley, it seems, made no attempt to strip to save himself before he drowned.

From an early age Shelley found it impossible to believe that the appearances of life could be the ultimate reality; in everything from the imagery of *Queen Mab*, to Tasso's handwriting, to the dome of many coloured glass in *Adonais*, to the pageant of *The Triumph of Life*, Shelley is searching for a meaning behind externals. Conversely it is because he was convinced that there was an ultimate meaning that he is so fascinated by the most shifting and evanescent manifestations: flames, winds, currents in water, clouds always changing, always renewing themselves, veils, light, never the same, but always the product of primal energy. These images—and they are images of something changeless—are merely details in his early poems but become central in many of his later ones, notably the important lyrics published with *Prometheus Unbound* (see Chapter 7). The 1818 sonnet 'Lift not the painted veil' shows Shelley in his depression expressing the search for truth and the desolation that search can bring:

> Lift not the painted veil which those who live
> Call life: though unreal shapes be pictured there,
> And it but mimic all we would believe
> With colours idly spread, —behind, lurk Fear
> And Hope, twin Destinies; who ever weave
> Their shadows, o'er the chasm, sightless and drear.
> I knew one who had lifted it—he sought,
> For his lost heart was tender, things to love,
> But found them not, alas! nor was there aught
> The world contains, the which he could approve.
> Through the unheeding many he did move,
> A splendour among shadows, a bright blot
> Upon this gloomy scene, a Spirit that strove
> For truth, and like the Preacher found it not.

That Shelley still associated himself with preaching, that in spite of despondency he believed in the future of mankind, is attested by *Prometheus Unbound* of which the first act was completed by the end of this year, 1818.

6

Prometheus Unbound

Already in *Queen Mab* Shelley had aspired to change the hearts of men and had seen this as the essential condition for political regeneration. Without it, revolution was bound to be bloody, merely substituting one form of oppression for another as in France. Even at twenty his impatience with Society was tempered by the realisation that change for the better would be a slow process. In *The Revolt of Islam* he had shown, in the failure of one revolution, both the possibility of hopeful change and the enormous forces of evil in political institutions and individuals militating against it. Any success in *The Revolt of Islam* is the result not of law or duty, but of love, of being humane. This was one reason why he disliked Christianity. The Church, he felt, had denied the gospel's message of love and had entrapped men in dogma, faith and superstition, negations of love and freedom. Of course Shelley acknowledged some laws—of logic, of nature or necessity. He was fascinated for instance by gravitation and atomic theory. In politics, too, in ethics, in psychology, there were laws: certain actions and emotions necessarily produce certain effects.

In the political poems we see Shelley exploring the public aspects of these unavoidable laws, in the more private poems he touches on their relation to the individual. In *Prometheus Unbound* he is concerned with the scope of man's freedom to think and act in relation to necessity—that is the nature of things over which man can have no control. The most extended conversation of the poem is concerned with the basic problem of the origin of evil. Depressed over the years by his failure to have any apparent influence on the political thinking of his age, he turned more and more to an exploration of the timeless laws underlying the repetitive patterns of human motivation and activity, political and private.

So, in *Prometheus Unbound*, his most complete expression of these cogitations, we have a poem which is both didactic and not didactic. It clearly hopes to inspire readers with a vision of the ideal, to teach men to use their imaginations, to inculcate hope for the future of man so that we can believe in and act upon the best that is within us, so that we may be guided by love rather than hate or self-interest. But it is no sort of political manifesto. Shelley said in the Preface that didactic poetry was his 'abhorrence'. *Prometheus Unbound* proposes no particular actions, its vision of a perfect future for man is a distant and evolving one, which acknowledges that there will always be disagreeables to contend with—chance, change, pain, mortality, guilt. It will have no immediate effect. In short it is not 'a reasoned system on the theory of human life' but a poem.

As a poem it is best approached as simply as possible, avoiding at first the 'abstruser musings' of the critics. It is rather daunting to be told by Mary Shelley that it requires a mind 'as subtle and penetrating as his own to understand the mystic meanings scattered throughout', and we may agree with Leigh Hunt that Shelley takes too little thought for the reader. Still, it is preferable to try to put poetical two and two together as best we may while we read, rather than to snatch 'mystic meanings' at second hand. The former at least stretches the imagination. The latter all too easily becomes passive acceptance of critical dogma, which would be as repugnant to Shelley as any other sort. Critics are accordingly banished to the bibliography.

However, a few facts and ideas can usefully be borne in mind— they are like coloured strands we come to recognise in the fabric of the poem. Several of them we have seen before in Shelley's poems and life, but here they appear together with fresh elements and in a new pattern, for in his 'lyric drama' Shelley was conscious of attempting something different from any other English poem. 'It is in my judgment', he wrote to his publisher, 'of a higher character than anything I have yet attempted; and it is perhaps less an imitation of anything that has gone before it'. Shelley's favourite dramatic form was ballet, and he also enjoyed some opera. Much of *Prometheus Unbound* is a sort of poetical ballet, more a verbal representation of music, light, and symbolic movement, than the conventional stuff of drama.

MYTH AND ACTION

Obviously the most important new strand in the poem is the myth of Prometheus itself. The story as Shelley found it in one of his favourite authors, Aeschylus, was as follows. Prometheus the Titan (whose name means Forethought) had helped Jupiter overthrow Saturn but has now incurred his anger having become the champion of men, stealing fire from the gods for them and teaching them arts and sciences. In punishment Prometheus is nailed to a rock to suffer torment. The daughters of the Titan Oceanus come to sympathise with him and Oceanus himself tries to persuade Prometheus to submit. Prometheus knows the secret on which Jupiter's reign depends (that Jupiter's son by Thetis whom he is about to marry will be greater than his father), but when Mercury is sent to demand the information from him, he refuses, and is hurled into the abyss, the Oceanides sharing his fate. The story is told in the *Prometheus Vinctus*. The final play in the trilogy has been lost though fragments show that Prometheus and Jupiter must ultimately have been reconciled. This sequel, in which presumably Prometheus buys freedom by telling the secret, so allowing Jupiter to avoid the fatal marriage and there-fore perpetuating his rule, Shelley emphatically rejected. 'I was averse from a catastrophe so feeble as that of reconciling the Champion with the Oppressor of mankind.' For Shelley Prometheus is 'the type of the highest perfection of moral and intellectual nature, impelled by the purest and truest motives to the best and noblest ends'. In some respects he is like Satan in *Paradise Lost* in his courageous opposition to omnipotent force but he is without Satan's flaws of envy, revenge and pride. As he hangs on the rock, in his willing submission to suffering for the sake of mankind he is also like Christ.

To become the type of moral perfection Prometheus must clearly undergo conflict. In Shelley's version of the story it is his will to forgive and pity, rather than hate, Jupiter, even while he opposes him, that brings about his own liberation and the downfall of the tyrant. The most important action of the poem takes place in Prometheus's first speech in Act I. Prometheus has been made wise by suffering. Still hanging in torment on the rock he finds that he no longer hates Jupiter but pities him for his inevitable fate:

> What ruin
> Will hunt thee undefended through wide Heaven!
> How will thy soul, cloven to its depth with terror,
> Gape like a hell within! I, 53–6

Prometheus knows that however far off it may be, the hour will come when Jupiter will fall and he himself will be unchained. He seeks to recall the curse he laid on Jupiter. The disinterested desire to recall the curse is in fact the precondition for Prometheus's physical liberation, because it is the proof of his freedom of mind. The rest of the drama follows from this self-liberation. It can bring about final freedom only if it is a continuing and developing state of mind. One sympathetic impulse is not enough. It must be tested.

After a passage of recapitulation by Earth, mother of Prometheus and all human and natural life, and by the Phantasm of Jupiter called forth to reiterate the curse laid on him by Prometheus, the temptation begins. The Earth is dejected that her son has apparently abandoned his fierce defiance of the tyrant, but Prometheus, while standing firm in his opposition to Jupiter, must yet keep himself clear of the taint of envy, hate and revenge. So Prometheus rejects the promise of 'voluptuous joy' among the gods if he tells the secret, and calmly faces the ferocity of furies straining at the leash to inflict new torments on him. When Mercury, Jupiter's somewhat unwilling messenger, warns him of the horror in store, he replies:

> I would not quit
> This bleak ravine, these unrepentant pains. I, 426–7

Here it is important to remember not only Prometheus's opposition to the omnipotent tyrant but his earlier role of knowledge-bringer to men. In his earlier, militantly vegetarian phase, Shelley had traced men's ills back to Prometheus's gift of fire under the cooking pot: 'Before the time of Prometheus mankind were exempt from suffering . . .' From the moment when he applied fire to culinary purposes 'his vitals were devoured by the vulture of disease. All vice arose from the ruin of healthful innocence.' Shelley has abandoned this over-simple view of the fall of man by the time he writes *Prometheus Unbound*.

Prometheus is an entirely admired figure, but Shelley does not dodge the difficulty that knowledge and aspiration inevitably bring suffering, that in human affairs good and evil are entwined. As in *Queen Mab* and *The Revolt of Islam*, what must be avoided is backward-looking remorse and paralysing self-contempt. Evil must be recognised and deplored, responsibility acknowledged, but Prometheus must look forward. The furies do their best to make him repent his past defiance. Greater than any physical torment is the anguish of mind caused by their recital of the suffering of men which they attribute to the knowledge which Prometheus has himself given them. The anguish of men will continue. He has brought them a consuming fever of 'hope, love, doubt, desire'. Any human good is inevitably followed by evil. The prime example of this is Christ:

> One came forth of gentle worth
> Smiling on the sanguine earth,
> His words outlived him, like swift poison
> Withering up truth, peace and pity.   I, 546–9

The perversion of Christ's love is the worst torment Prometheus has to undergo. He suffers most through others' agony. A fury sums up man's desolate condition, ending with Christ's words from the Cross:

> The good want power, but to weep barren tears.
> The powerful goodness want: worse need for them.
> The wise want love; and those who love want wisdom;
> And all best things are thus confused to ill.

> Many are strong and rich, and would be just,
> But live among their suffering fellow-men
> As if none felt: they know not what they do.   I, 625–31

These thoughts are like 'wingéd snakes' to Prometheus, but he pities those they do not torture. He sees Jupiter's works within himself. Shelley reminds us that it was Prometheus who gave power to Jupiter; as in *Queen Mab* tyrants are created by slavishness, as much as slaves by tyranny. This is one of the points in the poem where we are most clearly reminded that Shelley is using the myth not only to discuss political ideas of liberty and oppression, and philosophical ideas of good and evil, but also psychological ideas about human motives. Looked at in one way all the figures of the drama are aspects of the human mind.

This is again apparent when a chorus of comforting spirits replace the furies. In fact the subject-matter of their songs is not dissimilar to those of the furies: there is still conflict (1st spirit), enmity (2nd spirit), woe (3rd spirit), aspiration for the unattainable ideal (4th spirit). Ruin follows progress (5th spirit); pain inevitably accompanies love (6th spirit). But all these things are seen in a more hopeful light, they are growth points, buds from which better life may spring. The important thing is to have faith in moments of hope even when they are only memories. For Prometheus the one hope is love.

This brings us to Shelley's own innovations in the story of Prometheus. In Aeschylus, Prometheus is comforted by a chorus of the daughters of Oceanus. In *Prometheus Unbound* three appear. Panthea and Ione are by his side during his torture but he is separated from his loved one, their sister, Asia. Logically this must be so. They cannot be united in perfect love while hatred still lurks in his heart, but in their union perfect love will cast out all hate and fear. Since Asia is his necessary counterpart, Act II is devoted to her role in the drama. Characteristically with Shelley the perfect union of male and female is seen within a context of other tender but less intense relationships of brotherly and sisterly affection. The impulse for Asia's actions, which are to be essential for the final liberation of Prometheus, grows out of

87

Panthea's and Ione's empathy with Prometheus and their sister Asia. This is expressed in two dreams experienced but half forgotten by Panthea. When related to Asia, these recall her own similar dreams. They all combine to draw the two sisters on a quest to the cave of the mysterious power Demogorgon.

Two things seem important in the over-complicated dream action at this point. Firstly, Asia's quest springs out of a co-operative spirit of hope. In his Preface to the poem Shelley says that he believes such a spirit is abroad in his own age. 'The great writers of our own age are, we have reason to suppose, the companions and forerunners of some unimagined change in our social conditions or the opinions which cement it. The cloud of mind is discharging its collected lightning . . .' Secondly the coming change is 'unimagined', that is Asia and Panthea have to trust their impulse, they have to embark on the quest though they don't know where it will lead them. We are back with Shelley's insistence on the 'indefatigable hope, and long-suffering and long-believing courage' (Preface to *The Revolt of Islam*). In that they are ignorant of the outcome of their impulse, their actions are part of an inevitable tide bringing the future to birth. Shelley doesn't entirely abandon the *Queen Mab* idea of life inevitably, impersonally pressing forward, like flames round the marble column. But he does leave some room for free will. They choose to follow. They have the courage to look to the future.

Their journey lies first through a lush wooded landscape, populated by unseen, singing spirits and two more plain-spoken fawns. This leads to the grim entrance to Demogorgon's cave 'Like a volcano's meteor-breathing chasm'. Having ascended a pinnacle of rock they are in true romantic fashion called on to descend 'To the deep, to the deep,/Down, down'. In the depths sits the veiled form of Demogorgon. Even when the veil falls he has no definition, he is:

> a mighty darkness
> Filling the seat of power, and rays of gloom
> Dart round, as light from the meridian sun.
> —Ungazed upon and shapeless; neither limb,

> Nor form, nor outline; yet we feel it is
> A living Spirit.   II, *iv*, 2–7

Here is a strange combination of opposites. He is a positive force, he claims to be able to answer all the questions Asia dares ask, and in the third Act it is his thunderous arrival that unseats Jupiter. Yet he is defined by negatives and in the conversation which follows he tells Asia no more than she already really knows. When she asks who created the living world and everything in it he gives the orthodox answer: God. When she asks who created evil and pain he replies enigmatically: 'He reigns.' Again, that she may curse it she demands a name on which she can fix responsibility for evil. Again he replies: 'He reigns.' This prevents Asia from resorting to an unproductive, negative attitude—cursing doesn't do any good; it may temporarily relieve the feelings but it only confirms the curser in abjectness. The reply also makes Asia define the problem to herself. Each individual must work things out for himself. Evil presents two problems: where did it come from and what do we do about it? Fretting about the one doesn't help us solve the other. Asia recapitulates what she knows of the history of the world and man: after a paradisal period time emerged in the reign of Saturn, who still refused men knowledge and power. Knowledge of evil came to man when Prometheus gave power to Jupiter to dethrone Saturn. Where Saturn's reign denied men their birthright of knowledge, Jupiter's poured on them the bitter fruits of knowledge—toil, disease and war. As alleviation for his suffering Prometheus waked hope and love in man, gave him manual and verbal skills, medicine, astronomy, architecture. For all this he is still punished. Nevertheless Jupiter himself is as fearful as a slave. Who, then, is Jupiter's master? Jupiter, replies Demogorgon, is the 'supreme of living things'. Is—not must always be. Jupiter will be dethroned in Act III. Beyond that is mystery: 'the deep truth is imageless'.

To understand the workings of 'Fate, Time, Occasion, Chance and Change' wouldn't actually help Asia. The one positive Demogorgon affirms—that eternal love is exempt from the rule of Fate and Change—Asia has already known as intuition. Indeed the most important knowledge can only be learnt by experience, not by being told. 'Of such truths/Each to itself must be the oracle.' Experience, not dogma, is supreme. It is by coming to this conclusion, by being content with not knowing the unknowable, but trusting in the ultimate triumph of good, that Asia brings about the moment of Prometheus's release. There appears the shell-like chariot of the hour of Prometheus's liberation. Asia and Panthea ascend it and for the first time Asia, the embodiment of Love, is revealed in all her beauty. Panthea recalls how, Venus-like, she rose from the sea, standing on a shell, and love burst from her. For Asia love is as natural and ordinary as the air she breathes:

> Common as light is love,
> And its familiar voice wearies not ever.
> Like the wide heaven, the all-sustaining air,
> It makes the reptile equal to the God. II, *v*, 40–3

The giving and receiving of love is celebrated in two lyrics ending Act II.

The third Act presents the fall of Jupiter and the dawn of a new era for men. When Demogorgon's chariot thunders up Olympus, Jupiter is expecting him to use his power finally to trample out man's soul, spark of Promethean fire. Instead Jupiter finds that his own child Demogorgon is mightier than he, as he was mightier than Saturn. But the new era is not simply the replacement of one tyranny by another. After Jupiter, Demogorgon announces, 'The tyranny of heaven none may retain'. When the terrified oppressor asks the fearsome shape his name, Demogorgon replies: 'Eternity'. So as Jupiter and Demogorgon sink together to the abyss (tangled as the snake and eagle in *The Revolt of Islam*) temporal power is swallowed up in eternity. The revolutions of power are as nothing when viewed in relation to eternity. No wonder Jupiter would rather be judged by his enemy, Prometheus, full of human compassion, than be confronted by the impersonal power of Demogorgon, the logic of eternity.

Sea and Sun, Ocean and Apollo, recount the terror of his fall in scene ii and look to the beauty of a happier time, while in scene iii Hercules unbinds Prometheus:

> thus doth strength
> To wisdom, courage and long-suffering love,
> And thee, who art the form they animate,
> Minister like a slave,   III, *iii*, 1–4

Prometheus foresees a paradisal future in which he will withdraw with Asia and her sisters to a cave complete with trailing plants and leaping fountain. There they, unchanged themselves, will talk of 'time and change' and make 'strange combinations out of common things'—reminiscent of Cythna and her child innocently playing with shells in the cave in *The Revolt of Islam*. Though they are immortal, their paradise will be an evolving one as they search their 'unexhausted spirits', feel the 'murmured' pain of pity, and contemplate the immortal works of man—painting, sculpture, poetry, and 'arts, though unimagined yet to be'. These grow more beautiful as man becomes wise and kind.

Earth, too, becomes more beautiful and kind; joy renews her youth, and she feeds her children with healthful nourishment instead of disease and pain. When death comes to man, it is as comforting and natural as a mother calling her child; it is the lifting of the veil to a new life, compared to which mortal existence is death. Earth calls up the Spirit of the Earth, a winged child, to lead Prometheus to the destined cave.

Earth is the mother of all life on the globe from man to the mineral elements we think of as inanimate. The Spirit on the other hand is male, representing the planet in relation to the rest of the universe. Shelley sees the energy which rolls Earth on its course as an aspect of love—the young Spirit calls Asia (Love) 'Mother, dearest Mother'. In Act II he excitedly recounts the changes brought about in nature and man by the end of oppression. While the Spirit of the Earth's description is a simple visual one, the Spirit of the Hour presents the liberation in more abstract and intellectual terms. Man and woman move from unnatural oppression in which the heart may 'deny the *yes* it breathes' to one in which, free and equal, they are 'just, gentle and wise'. They do not vengefully tear down Kings' palaces, they merely disregard them. But their state is not a passive one, a perpetual feast of delights—they are still subject to 'chance, and death and mutability'. Though the pain of guilt is gone, man is still passionate.

Here Shelley's original version of *Prometheus Unbound* ended. But some months later he added a fourth Act, an extended paean in praise of love, which informs the whole world and illuminates history. The Spirit of the Earth, grown to maturity, reciprocates the love of the Moon. As Demogorgon finally assures us, Love in all its aspects, from the forces of gravity to human love and sacrifice, is the ultimate law of life:

> To suffer woes which Hope thinks infinite;
> To forgive wrongs darker than death or night;
>   To defy Power, which seems omnipotent;
> To love, and bear; to hope till Hope creates
> From its own wreck the thing it contemplates;
>   Neither to change, nor falter, nor repent;
> This, like thy glory, Titan, is to be
> Good, great and joyous, beautiful and free;
> This is alone Life, Joy, Empire, and Victory.   IV, 570–8

LANDSCAPE

Another important thread in the fabric of *Prometheus Unbound* is representation of the natural world. This is composed of several strands—landscapes, Shelley's knowledge and intuitions about the laws governing natural phenomena, and isolated details, particularly individual visual images. Of these landscape is probably the most immediately striking. Reference has already been made to the descriptions in Shelley's letters of 1818–19 of spectacular landscapes he was seeing for the first time. In the Preface he recalls that the poem was chiefly written 'upon the mountainous ruins of the Baths of Caracalla, among the flowery glades, and thickets of odoriferous blossoming trees, which are extended in ever winding labyrinths upon its immense platforms and dizzy arches suspended in the air. The bright blue sky of Rome, and the effect of the vigorous awakening spring in that divinest climate, and the new life with which it drenches the spirits even to intoxication, were the inspiration of this drama'. Certainly Shelley's fascination with light effects crops up again and again in the poem and we have several glimpses of ruins returned to nature. Other landscapes, too, find their place. An entry written by Shelley in Mary's journal for 1818 notes that the Alpine scenery is 'like that described in the Prometheus of Aeschylus; vast rifts and caverns in the granite precipices; wintry mountains with ice and snow above, the loud sounds of unseen waters within the caverns; and walls of toppling rocks, only to be scaled, as he describes, by the winged chariot of the Ocean Nymphs'. Once again we see Shelley fascinated by the deadness of the external landscape coupled with the indication of powerful life forces flowing beneath. This alpine landscape provides both background and metaphor for the suffering of Prometheus in Act I:

> The crawling glaciers pierce me with the spears
> Of their moon-freezing crystals, the bright chains
> Eat with their burning cold into my bones.   I, 31–3

Earth tremors 'wrench the rivets' from his 'quivering wounds'. Far below he can glimpse 'rock-embosomed lawns' where he once walked with Asia. As in *Mont Blanc* the pleasant and terrifying aspects of nature are inseparable.

The countryside round Naples where Shelley stayed at the end of 1818 also finds its way into *Prometheus Unbound*. A letter to Peacock shows the impact on him of a visit to Mount Vesuvius: 'The mountain is at present in a slight state of eruption; and a thick white smoke is perpetually rolled out, interrupted by enormous columns of an impenetrable black bituminous vapour, which is hurled up fold after fold, into the sky; and fiery stones are rained down from its darkness.' It was 'after the glaciers, the most impressive exhibition of the energies of nature I ever saw. It has not the immeasurable greatness, the overpowering magnificence, nor above all, the radiant beauty of the glaciers; but it has all their character of tremendous and irresistible

93

strength.' Aeschylus in the *Prometheus Bound* had described an eruption of Etna. This is the sort of power associated with Demogorgon. Mary Shelley calls him the 'Primal Power of the world' (and Boccaccio had located his dwelling underneath Etna). Shelley's description (II, *iii*, 1–10) of the entrance to Demogorgon's realm includes intoxicating vapours, presumably volcanic fumes.

To this desolate and awe-inspiring landscape Asia and Panthea come through a richly wooded pastoral scene, characteristic of the fertile belt surrounding a volcano. Again we have the conjunction of destruction and fertility. Demogorgon is both a destructive and a positive force. His subterranean power draws Asia to him; but it seems to need the combined wills of Prometheus, Ione, Panthea and Asia, finding expression in Asia's questions and Demogorgon's expected answers, to release it. They are, as it were, the gathering pressures that cause a volcanic eruption. This is what happens when the hour destined for Jupiter's overthrow arrives. At II, *iv*, 129 'The rocks are cloven', at l. 150 'That terrible shadow floats/Up from its throne, as may the lurid smoke/Of earthquake-ruined cities'. At III, *i*, 74, hell erupts on Jupiter: 'Let hell unlock/Its mounded oceans of tempestuous fire.'

SCIENTIFIC INTERESTS

Clearly, then, Shelley was interested in the causes and effects of such natural phenomena as volcanoes and earthquakes. He did not think of landscape only in aesthetic or symbolic terms, but related it to its determining geological factors. His fascination with all aspects of nature that seem most instinct with fluctuating life continues—with light and sound waves, with electricity, with winds, with clouds and vapours. His speculations include life on other planets, the origin of meteors, which he imagines are the result of the exhalation of gases from water, and electropropulsion. He envisages some sort of atomic life; Panthea seems to use X-ray beams, making 'bare the secrets of the earth's deep heart'; in Act IV also the love between earth and moon is expressed in terms of gravitational forces as well as visually; a stanza of one of the earth's lyrics (IV, 418–22) prophesies scientific advances for men such as he had propounded to Hogg in Oxford days—electric motors, aeroplanes, space travel and seismology.

Some of these passages are difficult to follow, but the obscurity arises more from Shelley's attempts at exactness, than from vagueness. Partly they are baffling in the way that a non-scientist finds scientific theory baffling. Some of the ideas are mistaken, but some seem genuine intuitions about the way in which scientific thought was to develop. What is important poetically is that Shelley sees science and art progressing together with a moral advance in man. He sees all the disparate forces of nature as ultimately part of a whole. This unity to which man, too, is gradually working, can be summed up in one word—Love. In *The Revolt of Islam* 'Love is celebrated everywhere as the sole law which should govern the moral world'; in *Prometheus Unbound* it is also seen as the mainspring of the universe.

ISOLATED IMAGES

While some of the extended scientific observations or theories are apparently vague and perplexing, *Prometheus Unbound* does contain some isolated images which impress with the authority of simple, economical expression. Some of these have a delicacy particularly characteristic of Shelley, caught in a line or two, as in Panthea's description of Mercury's departure:

> See where the child of Heaven, with wingéd feet
> Runs down the slanted sunlight of the dawn.   I, 437–8

Or of the moon spirit:

> Its plumes are as feathers of sunny frost,
> Its limbs gleam white, through the wind-flowing folds
> Of its white robe, woof of ethereal pearl.   IV, 221–3

Or Asia's comparison of her soul to:

> an enchanted boat
> Which, like a sleeping swan, doth float
> Upon the silver waves of thy sweet singing.   II, *v*, 72–4

Some of these richly evocative passages are more extended as in the song of the sixth spirit in Act I:

> Ah, sister! Desolation is a delicate thing:
>   It walks not on the earth, it floats not on the air,
> But treads with lulling footstep, and fans with silent wing
>   The tender hopes which in their hearts the best and gentlest bear;
>
> Who, soothed to false repose by the fanning plumes above
>   And the music-stirring motion of its soft and busy feet,
> Dream visions of aëreal joy, and call the monster, Love,
>   And wake, and find the shadow Pain, as he whom now we greet.
>
> > > > > > I, 772–9

Or Ocean's account of his underwater realm:

> The loud deep calls me home even now to feed it
> With azure calm out of the emerald urns
> Which stand for ever full beside my throne.
> Behold the Nereids under the green sea,
> Their wavering limbs borne on the wind-like stream,
> Their white arms lifted o'er their streaming hair
> With garlands pied and starry sea-flower crowns,
> Hastening to grace their mighty sister's joy.   III, *ii*, 41–8

This description ends to the sound of waves with a line that suddenly widens the picturesqueness of classical representations of the god to a sense of the sea's potentially destructive power and mystery, and a suggestion of universal longing for repose: 'It is the unpastured sea hungering for calm.' There is a breadth in this line which reminds us of Shelley's admiration for Milton. He has caught the same impulse as Dalila's in *Samson Agonistes:* 'But winds to seas are reconciled at length/And sea to shore.' A clarity and toughness that is sometimes denied Shelley appears in brief images, some non-visual—'cold, hollow talk/Which makes the heart deny the *yes* it breathes'—some visual. Earth's recital of the evils afflicting her children is vividly brought to life:

> Blue thistles bloomed in cities; foodless toads
> Within voluptuous chambers panting crawled. I, 170–1

By contrast the Spirit of the Earth's delight in the regeneration of man is epitomised by the image of two kingfishers:

> I cannot tell my joy, when o'er a lake
> Upon a drooping bough with nightshade twined,
> I saw two azure halcyons clinging downward
> And thinning one bright bunch of amber berries,
> With quick long beaks, and in the deep there lay
> Those lovely forms imaged as in a sky. III, iv, 78–83

Though in the description of Prometheus's cave, for instance, there is exotic vegetation—'bright golden globes/Of fruit, suspended in their own green heaven'—Shelley is as successful when he uses clouds 'dark with the rain new buds are dreaming of' or the commonest shrubs of English hedgerows:

> In the atmosphere we breathe,
> As buds grow red when the snow-storms flee,
> From Spring gathering up beneath,
> Whose mild winds shake the elder brake,
> And the wandering herdsmen know
> That the white-thorn soon will blow. I, 790–5

This is a chorus assured of the signs of regeneration. Another sign is the terse account of 'one who gave an enemy/His plank, then plunged aside to die'. Other indications are the dreams of the poet. Here Shelley combines the sense of the artist's longing for an ideal with his need for and delight in the actual:

> Nor seeks nor finds he mortal blisses,
> But feeds on the aëreal kisses
> Of shapes that haunt thought's wildernesses.
> He will watch from dawn to gloom
> The lake-reflected sun illume
> The yellow bees in the ivy-bloom,
> Nor heed nor see, what things they be;
> But from these create he can
> Forms more real than living man,
> Nurslings of immortality! I, 740–9

This is put more concisely in relation to sculpture and painting in IV, 411–12: 'Through the cold mass/Of marble and of colour his dreams pass.' Both of these quotations have a sense of the mystery of artistic creativity, itself a response to the mystery of universal creation.

Indeed the greatness of *Prometheus Unbound* lies in Shelley's ability to find pictures for spiritual insights, and to speak with resonant assurance of truths which most of us are too timid to utter but which, at least temporarily, he makes us believe. Some of these have the conciseness of epigram: love 'makes the reptile equal to the God'; 'familiar acts are beautiful through love'; 'He gave man speech, and speech created thought/ Which is the measure of the Universe'. Two more extended passages carry immediate conviction because they are so closely related to the visual background of the poem. Mercury envisages eternity as a great abyss, reflecting both Prometheus's actual situation hanging on a precipice, but also the common experience of the mind's recoil from the infinite:

> Yet pause, and plunge
> Into Eternity, where recorded time,
> Even all that we imagine, age on age,
> Seems but a point, and the reluctant mind
> Flags wearily in its unending flight,
> Till it sink, dizzy, blind, lost, shelterless.

I, 416–21

Asia dramatically compares an avalanche to truth:

> Hark! the rushing snow!
> The sun-awakened avalanche! whose mass,
> Thrice sifted by the storm, had gathered there
> Flake after flake, in heaven-defying minds
> As thought by thought is piled, till some great truth
> Is loosened, and the nations echo round,
> Shaken to their roots, as do the mountains now. II, *iii*, 36–42

Both these examples contain what one might call self-evident human truths, ideas any reader can easily accept. But Shelley also treads more mystical paths as in the Earth's account of the separate existence of thoughts and ideas apart from the thinker:

> Ere Babylon was dust
> The Magus Zoroaster, my dead child,
> Met his own image walking in the garden.
> That apparition, sole of men, he saw.
> For know there are two worlds of life and death:
> One that which thou beholdest; but the other
> Is underneath the grave, where do inhabit
> The shadows of all forms that think and live
> Till death unite them and they part no more.   I, 191–9

The reference to the eighth-century B.C. Persian religious leader suggests an awareness of the oneness of human spiritual experience, irrespective of time and space. Shelley had visions and hallucinations himself, and shortly before his death saw his wraith. The passage also underlines Shelley's sense of the potency of thought, a sense encouraged by his concentrated reading of Plato. For Shelley the appearances of the finite world though fascinating could not be the ultimate reality—hence Earth's assurance that 'Death is the veil which those who live call life./ They sleep and it is lifted'.

Mary Shelley's comment that he believed that 'mankind had only to will that there should be no evil and there would be none' oversimplifies, but it is basically true. Man is capable of being greater than his circumstances because temporal life is not the only life. As Wordsworth puts it, 'Our destiny, our being's heart and home,/Is with infinitude, and only there'. At the same time Shelley was humanistic, believing, again with Wordsworth, that this world is 'the place where, in the end/We find our happiness, or not at all!' This hopefulness about the possibility of revolutionising man's existence upon earth, and about love (which not only occurs in human life but is also a universal, timeless principle) is the basis of the exhilaration of *Prometheus Unbound*.

7

Sky Poems: Poems published with *Prometheus Unbound*, 1820

The years 1819 and 1820 were astonishingly productive for Shelley. *Prometheus Unbound* had been started in 1818 at Este, continued at Rome in the early months of 1819, and the fourth Act was added some months later at Florence. His one complete drama, *The Cenci*, started in May, was finished by early August and he was also thinking about *Charles I*, taken up again a couple of years later (see Chapter 9). Meanwhile in England the political situation was worsening, and Shelley responded with a series of political poems and an essay, *A Philosophical View of Reform*, begun in November 1819 (see Chapter 8).

Once again Shelley's own life was distressful. Godwin was pressing him for more money while abusing him to Mary. She was pregnant again, and so upset by her father's letters that she asked Shelley to keep them from her. Of his gifts to Godwin Shelley said in a letter to Hunt, 'I have bought bitter experience with £4,700'. June 1819 brought another shattering blow in the death of three-year-old William Shelley. William was old enough to be quite a personality, so the loss must have been yet greater than that of the baby Clara. This time however, though Mary withdrew into her desolation (only somewhat alleviated by the birth in November 1819 of Percy Florence Shelley, the one child who survived into adulthood), Shelley managed to overcome his grief in poetic activity. The sad shorter poems written after Clara's death looked towards death. But the poems to be discussed in this chapter, written in 1819 and 1820, and published with *Prometheus Unbound* in October 1820, celebrate life. They are not escapist poems, since sadness, change and death are prominent elements. But these are seen as part of a larger pattern of life. In basic attitude they are closely allied to *Prometheus Unbound*. Several also share its fascination with the sky.

The shortest of these sky poems is the *Ode to Heaven*. Three spirits in turn attempt definitions of heaven, the second modifying the first, the third 'correcting' that. True, the three are called a chorus by Shelley, suggesting that the three views are equally important aspects of the subject, but the poem has a neat 'turn' at the end which gives a sense of progression. The first spirit sees heaven as an embodiment of the eternal; the vastness of heaven appears like a dome canopying the past and the future of the earth. But it is more than a roof, it is also the immeasurable expanses of space containing other galaxies and solar systems. No wonder then that heaven is spoken of as a deity, the Power 'which is the glass/Wherein man his nature sees'. While man is essentially ephemeral, heaven is constant. Here the second spirit interrupts. The first spirit's view, though it seemed all-embracing, is too limited. Heaven is only the beginning, 'the mind's first chamber', 'the portal of the grave' compared to a 'world of new delights' which must be beyond. Such assurance is swept away by the third spirit who compares heaven to the evanescence of a drop of dew:

> Constellated suns unshaken,
> Orbits measureless, are furled
> In that frail and fading sphere,
> With ten millions gathered there,
> To tremble, gleam and disappear.   ll. 50–4

Once again we have Shelley looking beyond the visible, attracted to an image of the constant but fascinated by the idea of fluctuation or process. Of the most famous of the other lyrics included in the volume, the ode *To a Skylark*, *The Cloud*, and the *Ode to the West Wind*, the first is an expression of a continuous joyousness —the skylark seems to inhabit an eternal realm. The others celebrate process.

The Shelleys went to Florence in October so that Mary could

be in the care of a reliable doctor for the birth of her baby in November. Recalling his walk one day in a wood skirting the River Arno, Shelley tells us that the *Ode to the West Wind* was inspired by the tempestuous wind 'at once wild and animating' which was 'collecting the vapours which pour down the autumnal rain'. Here at last an idea that appeared in details of earlier poems becomes central. The wind, destroyer and life-bringer, the dead autumn leaves eventually fertilising the ground, had been used as similes or metaphors in *Queen Mab* and *The Revolt of Islam*. Now they have a poem all to themselves. Shelley's instinctive attraction to these images, previously a sort of signature at the side of the picture, is here fully incorporated into the composition. The poet is both contrasted and potentially identified with the wind. Shelley manages to find a structure in which the comparison seems natural, because he immediately appeals to common experience—the exhilaration of feeling autumn wind, having one's lungs filled, of being almost bowled along by it. He captures this feeling by the words he chooses but primarily by his rhythmic control. It is because the poem is very highly wrought that it seems natural. Like the force of the prevailing wind which nevertheless includes eddies, the poem sweeps cumulatively through long fourteen-line rhythms. In the first three stanzas this exactly echoes the sense; each is an invocation to the wind seen in different aspects, each leads to the gasped appeal 'oh hear'. Trying to read the poem aloud proves what a brilliant imitation this is—one almost needs the lung-power of the wind itself. Some readers will feel that the poet's concern with his own predicament in Stanza 4 is intrusive:

> I fall upon the thorns of life! I bleed!
> A heavy weight of hours has chained and bowed
> One too like thee: tameless, and swift, and proud.

But this may be because Shelley's experience, exceptional though it was in the intensity of its hopes, distresses and disappointments, is more like our own experience than we care to admit. There are few people who do not at some time or other fasten on an aspect of nature as an image of the greater freedom or power they long for and in their headier moments believe they might achieve. Few therefore do not, momentarily at least, indulge in self-pity. From this most of us subside into 'philosophic' acceptance of our unfree, unimportant destinies. Shelley is exceptional in what he feels, not so much in Stanza 4 as in Stanza 5, where two strands from his earlier poetry come together. In the last stanza of the *Hymn to Intellectual Beauty* Shelley had noticed a serenity at the end of the day, and the end of the year, which he linked with the Spirit leading him to love all forms that embodied it and all human kind (see p. 53).

In *Ode to the West Wind* it is the 'deep autumnal tone' de-rived from the forest, and the falling of the poet's own 'leaves' that will be part of the inspiration 'to quicken a new birth'. The other strand is the by now familiar one of the 'long-believing courage' that may be the 'trumpet of a prophecy'. The excep-tional heroes of other poems, Laon and Cythna, or Prometheus, all suffering for a cause, had shown that suffering could be en-nobling and ultimately life-giving. In the *Ode* the poet is not exceptional. The thorns of life are ordinary, built into the life process. But he is unusual in his belief that something positive might be made out of this common experience. However, too many disappointments lay behind Shelley, and he had too many fears as well as hopes about the future, to be complacent. So the poem ends not with an assertion but with a question:

> O Wind,
> If Winter comes, can Spring be far behind?

It is because of this that the poem impresses; Shelley is celebrating the life process, which is also the death process, and the two as-pects are finely balanced. He has not come to an easy conclusion but appears to be actually in the process of working towards some sort of equilibrium. This he achieves because he suggests the way we all live on several planes at once, having short-term and long-term thoughts, spontaneous impulses and general philosophical tendencies. Here the poet is revealing an immediate reaction to a particular situation and an underlying habit of thought. So the west wind is both a symbol and not a symbol: a symbol for the life-giving thoughts that one generation passes on to the next, even after death, but also simply the west wind blowing through the Florentine woods or wherever the reader happens to be. Shelley is as interested in the wind for its own sake as for the way he can use it in his poem.

The first three stanzas are full of precise observation and imaginative evocation of cause and effect in nature, on the earth, in the air and beneath the water. Shelley notices different kinds of clouds and is enough of a weatherman to know that storms will follow. In a letter quoted in Chapter 5 we had seen him peering under the water of the Bay of Naples; here he is fascinated by the prismatic effect of water, and by the unity of nature seen in the sympathy of under-water plants to more easily perceived seasonal changes on land. And writing to Godwin in 1817 he claimed to be able to communicate 'the conceptions which result from considering either the moral or the material universe as a whole.' Here the unity provokes longing for oneness with nature, a oneness almost experienced in boyhood 'when to outstrip thy skiey speed/Scarce seemed a vision', and passionately expressed in 'Be thou me, impetuous one'. Once more, however, we see Shelley reaching beyond self-fulfilment. No matter how self-absorbed he sometimes was, from an early age he tried to eliminate 'the burr that will stick to one', the self. Even aged eighteen he was 'sick to Death at the name of *self*'. In the *Ode*, satisfaction for the self in being one with nature is not the end, but rather the beginning of moral usefulness to his fellow human beings.

The mood of the autumnal *Ode to the West Wind* is exhilarated but sober, reflecting recent sorrow as well as hope for the future. The mood of *The Cloud* is joyous, and the ode *To a Skylark* is more whimsical, though it by no means excludes pain. Both belong to 1820. There is no need to belabour the point that Shelley was fascinated by the sky, the planets, clouds and atmospheric changes. *The Cloud* is a gleeful expression of this delight. The simple device of writing in the first person would have been novel to his first readers. It has the merit of directness. The cloud speaks for itself. The reader may if he chooses see the cloud as a symbol of some of Shelley's deepest feelings about the relationship between transience and permanence. The poem culminates in the line 'I change but I cannot die', and this idea is reflected in the verse form, where alliteration, assonance and the sense of words make subtle variations on an insistent rhyme and rhythm. But the cloud takes pleasure simply in being itself, it doesn't concern itself with being a symbol. If natural phenomena had not first and foremost been important to Shelley for their own sake, for their beauty and liveliness, they couldn't have been important to him as *forms* of life or expressions of something beyond themselves, whether he calls that Necessity, Power, Intellectual Beauty or Love. The poem has roughnesses where rhyme seems clumsy and syntax, particularly the use of pronouns, less clear than it might be. But the best moments contain some of Shelley's most vivid observations—the whitening of the plain under hail (l. 10), the moon and stars peering through the rent in the cloud cover in Stanza 4, the belt of cloud round the sun and moon (ll. 59–60).

Shelley identifies with the cloud, but his separateness from the bird is the main point of the ode *To a Skylark* as is Keats's separateness from the nightingale in his ode. For both Keats and Shelley the songs of the unseen birds represent something more permanent than man, and happier. Each poet envies the spontaneity of his bird and its ignorance of pain. But whereas when the nightingale flies away Keats is left desolate scarcely knowing whether it was real, Shelley returns from recognition of the disadvantages of man's conscious intelligence, to delight in the sheer joy the bird seems to embody. Typically he turns to the future, even though it is a hypothetical one. If only he could learn gladness from the bird the world would listen to his song too. Though more modest here than in earlier poems—he is only the centre of attention for three lines in the last stanza—he is nearer to Coleridge than to Keats. At the end of *Kubla Khan* Coleridge imagined the power and poetic magic he would possess if he could recapture his vision. The difference here is that Shelley has a better chance of recapturing gladness since he is responding not to a unique dream but to one of the blessed commonplaces of nature. Even if the poet has put an interpretation on the song of the bird which a naturalist might not accept, at the end of the poem he is still listening, and the bird is real. So though it is a poem of yearning, though it recognises that 'our sincerest laughter/With some pain is fraught', it is predominantly a poem of joy. The lark is part of the evidence of things not seen, and, simply, its song sounds happy and at one with the rest of nature:

> From rainbow clouds there flow not
> Drops so bright to see
> As from thy presence showers a rain of melody.   ll. 33–5

One of the signs of Shelley's growing maturity as a poet is that he becomes less intrusive in his own poems. This is not to say that they are not intensely personal, or that anyone else could have written his later poems, and in short lyrics in particular he continues to use the first personal pronoun a good deal. But he represents aspects of human emotion that can be generally shared. The exception to this, *Epipsychidion*, in which he is largely autobiographical, was a poem he grew to dislike. So though some critics identify Shelley with the Sensitive Plant, in the poem also published with *Prometheus Unbound*, it is at face value a presentation of the processes of nature at work in a garden.

The first part describes the beauty of the flowers and the unobtrusive *mimosa pudica*, which is sensitive to light and touch. Shelley is in fanciful mood as he lists the flowers and attributes human emotions to the mimosa: 'It desires what it has not, the Beautiful.' A new friend, Mrs. Mason, ex-pupil of Mary Wollstencraft, may have been the model for the gentle gardener of part 2, so sympathetic to all forms of life that, instead of exterminating 'all killing insects and gnawing worms/And things of obscene and unlovely forms', she merely transported them in a basket to the wild, where she made sure they had enough to eat. If based on Mrs. Mason this Eve-like figure was not young. 'You will think', Shelley rather engagingly wrote to Hunt, 'it is my fate either to find or imagine some Lady of 45 very unprejudiced and philosophical ... with enchanting manners and a disposition rather to like me in every town that I inhabit.' And the garden is no Eden. Abruptly in the last line of the second part the gardener dies. The garden mourns as the year draws to its end. A nightmarish winter scene succeeds. Shelley gives all too accurate a description of the demise of the sensitive plant (as anyone who has tried to grow *mimosa pudica* in England will testify):

> The Sensitive Plant, like one forbid,
> Wept, and the tears within each lid
> Of its folded leaves, which together grew,
> Were changed to a blight of frozen glue.　　ll. 78–81

Only weeds and fungi seem to revive the following spring in the choked garden. The hope that the garden and the lady have in reality not passed away since, however much we change, 'there is no death and change' for love, beauty and delight, is expressed, not as a conviction in this poem, but as a hesitant comfort, 'a modest creed and yet/Pleasant if one considers it'.

There are two other longish poems in the collection. *A Vision of the Sea* is more nightmarish than dreamlike with some extraordinary surrealistic incident and detail, and at ll. 11–22 a striking impressionist description of a Turneresque storm at sea. The *Ode to Liberty* has obvious links with *Prometheus Unbound* at l. 183 when the pent forces of liberty about to burst forth are compared to volcanic eruption, Vesuvius wakening Etna. It also recalls the *Ode to the West Wind*, in that the Spanish uprising is seen as a possible sign of political Spring. However, in its public nature it is more closely allied to the political poems to be discussed in the next chapter.

8

Politics, 1819 onwards

Shelley's political writings of 1819 and 1820 range from his most
mature pamphlet, *A Philosophical View of Reform*, to the abstract
and declamatory *Ode to Liberty*, to burlesque and satire in
Swellfoot the Tyrant, *The Mask of Anarchy* and *Peter Bell the Third*.

In the aftermath of the Napoleonic wars, political unrest was
growing with the pressures of increasing industrialisation and
with the working majority of the population unrepresented in
Parliament. The Government had taken repressive measures;
reform or revolution seemed inevitable. The situation exploded
on 16 August, 1819. Henry Hunt, the radical orator, was due to
address a reform meeting calling for universal suffrage, in St.
Peter's Field, Manchester. Sixty to a hundred thousand people
from Manchester and neighbouring towns, carrying banners,
were peacefully assembled. On the orders of the terrified magis-
trates the Yeomanry stood by to arrest Hunt and disperse the
crowd. Hunt had scarcely begun to address a quiet and attentive
audience when this ill-disciplined force of amateur soldiers
seized him and charged into the crowd, sabres drawn. Legally
such a meeting could only be closed after the Riot Act had been
read and an hour had elapsed allowing the crowd to disperse. If
the Riot Act was actually read nobody at the meeting seems to
have heard it. Eleven unarmed citizens were killed, and four
hundred or so wounded, either sabred or trampled by horses.

The 'Peterloo Massacre' produced a storm of protest. When
Shelley heard the news he responded with *The Mask of Anarchy*
(though Leigh Hunt, to whom it was sent, did not publish it till
1832). The poem is a mask (masque) in the sense of a procession
of allegorical figures. Anarchy (meaning misgovernment)—

'I am God, and King and Law'—is attended by Murder, in the form of Lord Castlereagh, Fraud (Lord Eldon), Hypocrisy (Lord Sidmouth), and a train of hated bishops, lawyers, peers, informers and spies. Oppression derives from force and fraud, represented by the Tower and the Bank. Shelley believed the abolition of the regular army and the National Debt were necessary reforms. At the time there was little cause for optimism. So Hope is 'a maniac maid', looking more like Despair. The Men of England are called on to rouse themselves from the slavery of forced labour and the fraudulent system of paper money that tends to devalue that labour. After all, they are many; those with the privileges, wealth and power but few. Freedom consists in bread, warmth, clothes, shelter, equality before the law, religious toleration, and peace. The way to achieve this is through knowledge, and the exercise of rational and artistic powers. Courage, patience and gentleness are essential. Shelley envisages a vast assembly of the oppressed and the enlightened to demand reform. Violence on the part of the ruling power is likely, but must be countered with passive resistance. Doubtless there will be martyrs. But where there is steadfast purpose change is inevitable:

> Rise like lions after slumber
> In unvanquishable number,
> Shake your chains to earth like dew
> Which in sleep had fallen on you—
> Ye are many—they are few.   ll. 151-5

The force of the poem derives from its simple form, directness, and icy control.

> I met Murder on the way—
> He had a mask like Castlereagh—
> Very smooth he looked, yet grim;
> Seven blood-hounds followed him:
>
> All were fat; and well they might
> Be in admirable plight,
> For one by one, and two by two
> He tossed them human hearts to chew
> Which from his wide cloak he drew.

Next came Fraud, and he had on,
Like Eldon, an ermined gown;
His big tears, for he wept well,
Turned to mill-stones as they fell.

And the little children, who
Round his feet played to and fro,
Thinking every tear a gem,
Had their brains knocked out by them.   ll. 5–21

Similar ideas are expressed in a number of shorter poems such as *Lines Written during the Castlereagh Administration* or *Similes for two Political Characters*, where those in power are seen as death-bringers. A parody of the National Anthem stresses the need for liberty in the hearts of men. The plight of the labouring classes is again defined in *Song to the Men of England*—they are duped into forging their own chains by selling their labour cheaply. Shelley sums up the situation in this sonnet, *England in 1819*:

An old, mad, blind, despised, and dying king,—
Princes, the dregs of their dull race, who flow
Through public scorn,—mud from a muddy spring,—
Rulers, who neither see, nor feel, nor know
But leech-like to their fainting country cling,
Till they drop, blind in blood, without a blow,—
A people starved and stabbed in the untilled field,—
An army, which liberticide and prey
Makes as a two-edged sword to all who wield,—
Golden and sanguine laws which tempt and slay;
Religion Christless, Godless—a book sealed;
A Senate,—Time's worst statute unrepealed,—
Are graves, from which a glorious Phantom may
Burst, to illumine our tempestuous day.

That Shelley thought England was at a time of crisis and that he was doubtful of the outcome is indicated by the last two lines. What at first seems characteristic optimism after a catalogue of ills is made hesitant by the 'may' in the penultimate line.

The 'old, mad, blind, despised and dying king' George III was succeeded by the old, fat Prince Regent, who had not endeared himself to radicals by writing to the Manchester Yeomanry congratulating them on their conduct of the Hunt meeting. In 1820 George IV was trying to get rid of his long-separated wife Queen Caroline. Now Lord Castlereagh placed the 'Green Bag' containing charges against her on the table of the House of Commons and demanded an inquiry into her conduct. After three months the bill was withdrawn, as it could command a majority of only nine. This is the political background to *Oedipus Tyrannus* or *Swellfoot the Tyrant*. Though Shelley did not think the affair of 'this vulgar cook maid they call a Queen' of great importance, he was glad enough of an opportunity of attacking the King. He hit on the idea of a burlesque drama on the subject one day when, as Mary Shelley tells us, his reading of his *Ode to Liberty* to some friends was 'riotously accompanied by the grunting of a quantity of pigs' brought to a fair in the square beneath their windows. In the drama the pigs represent the people, the gluttonous privileged porkers lapping up rich hogwash, and the ignorant, oppressed masses who only get water and straw, just enough to keep them in existence to provide bacon for their rulers. Obsessed with food, but worshipping Famine for others, gouty Swellfoot (George IV) is alarmed by the return of the Queen, Iona, round whom flock the disaffected. His ministers fear an oracle which says:

> choose reform or civil war!
> When through the streets, instead of hare with dogs,
> A Consort Queen shall hunt a King with Hogs,
> Riding on the Ionian Minotaur.   I, 113–16

The Queen, like Io in the Greek legend, has been pursued by the gadfly of the Milan Commission (which looked into her conduct), and the man who set it up, Sir John Leech. The King would like her arrested and executed. But for this Purganax (Lord Castlereagh) would have to assemble and corrupt a jury of pigs. Besides, Wellington in the person of Laoctonos, bibber of blood and claret, reports that some of the army sides with the Queen. Even Lord Eldon's affecting oratory (Shelley calls him Dakry or 'weeper') fails to arouse the swine against the Queen. Then Mammon, father of Banknotia (paper money), hits on the idea of the Green Bag filled with gadfly's venom, the Leech's vomit and ratsbane. Showing his scorn of the pigs' intelligence, Mammon declares that if guilty the Queen will become deformed, if innocent will be transfigured to an angel 'showering down blessings in the shape of comfits'.

Act II contains an example of Castlereagh's oratory and innuendo, when in addressing the assembly of boars he ostentatiously avoids using the word 'adultery'. After some demur, but lured by the vision of comfits, they favour the test of the Green Bag, which is duly fixed for the day of the feast of Famine. At the great moment, while shamming saintly innocence, the Queen seizes the bag and tips the contents over Swellfoot and his court, who are transformed into animals. The figure of the Goddess Famine is replaced by the Ionian Minotaur, nimbly translated by Shelley as 'John Bull'. The play ends with the victorious Queen, with attendant pig-hounds, fulfilling the oracle by joyously mounting the Bull to hunt her enemies.

Into this simple burlesque structure Shelley deftly fits references to his by now familiar political concerns. The starving pigs bear the chief burdens of taxation; any voice raised in protest is regarded as seditious; the pigs seem fierce because they are oppressed, swollen, not with food as their rulers declare (and as artists such as Gilray depicted them), but with the dropsy of starvation. The system of public credit and paper money inevitably leads to the breeding of gallows fodder. The ruling class find it convenient to accept the theory of Malthus (1766–1834), that the evils of the poor were unavoidable since they arose from an excess of population which could only be checked by war, poverty and disease. Even the double standard of morality for men and women is touched on when the pigs suggest that the King might well undergo a test too:

> I vote Swellfoot and Iona
>   Try the magic test together
> Whenever royal spouses bicker
> Both should try the magic liquor.

For a predominantly serious writer who only a year or so

previously had written in a letter of the 'withering and perverting spirit of comedy' and who had declared, according to Hogg, that 'there can be no complete regeneration of mankind till laughter be put down', Shelley doesn't do too badly. He clearly enjoys the piggishness of the pigs. His verbal humour ranges from comic rhyme, as in the last quotation, to oratorical parody (and it's good to see him parodying himself in the song of the gadfly). He includes jolly visual fantasy, as when Mammon imagines the pigs holding the flaps of each other's ears in their teeth 'To catch the coming hail of comfits in', and cunning quibble, as in Swellfoot's first speech. Here 'kingly paunch' is primarily visual, the sign of complacent princely splendour, but it also reminds us that in Shelley's constant view kings are inevitably paunchy and diseased since they draw food away from the people and suffer surfeit themselves. Lines 9–10 refer not only to the King's inherent worthlessness but suggest his bald head on his bloated body, O upon O.

Swellfoot is a rumbustious joke but it is also a serious one since, as Mary said, it shows 'sympathy for the sorrows of humanity and indignation against its oppressors'. A similar mixture of fun and seriousness had characterised his earlier parody, *Peter Bell the Third*, also partly political in content. The first *Peter Bell* was a poem by Wordsworth, published in April 1819. The second was a skit on it by J. H. Reynolds. Shelley had long held a double view of Wordsworth. As Mary Shelley says in her note, he read his poetry constantly and 'taught others to appreciate its beauties'. But he deplored Wordsworth's growing conservatism as he had Southey's. 'What a beastly and pitiful worm that Wordsworth!' he exclaimed in a letter to Godwin in 1818, 'That such a man should be such a poet.' It was almost inevitable, Shelley thought, that Wordsworth's abandonment of liberal principles should bring a failure of imagination and the poet's unforgivable sin—dullness. So though *Peter Bell the Third* is jocular 'perhaps no one will believe in anything in the shape of a joke from me', said Shelley—it is modified by an understanding of the nature of Wordsworth's genius and regret for its eclipse. The story is of a man of out-standing powers selling his soul to the *status quo*.

In Wordsworth's poem an itinerant seller of pots repents of his sins (polygamy, wanting to steal an ass, and hitting it when he finds it not worth stealing), through finding, after many stanzas, a drowned man, owner of the donkey. The faithful animal leads him to the man's faithful family. At this point Shelley takes up the story. Peter falls mortally sick and the Devil who has bought him for half a crown carries him off to the fashionable Hell of Grosvenor Square. The third section is a lively account of the self-seeking, self-damning London populated by Shelley's pet hates.

Wordsworth's originality—he had 'though unimaginative/An apprehension, clear intense/Of his mind's work'—was, Shelley suggests, given life by the influence of Coleridge. Thus:

> . . . Peter's verse was clear, and came
>   Announcing from the frozen hearth
> Of a cold age, that none might tame
> The soul of that diviner flame
>   It augured to the Earth:
>
> Like gentle rains, on the dry plains
>   Making that green which late was gray,
> Or like the sudden moon that stains
> Some gloomy chamber's window-panes
>   With a broad light like day.   ll. 433–42

So he almost escapes the Devil's clutches, who nevertheless thinks of a ruse to damn him. Naturally any good poet is attacked by the critics, so the Devil sends poor Peter a parcel of adverse reviews which soon bring him to heel: 'he grew dull, harsh, sly, unrefined'. The Devil is certain of his soul when the re-viewers turn kind (ll. 619–23). Corrupted by praise and a sine-cure, Peter incurs the double damnation of dullness:

> His state was like that of the immortal
>   Described by Swift—no man could bear him.   ll. 711–12

As dullness spreads for miles around him, by implication enveloping Southey who lived twelve miles off, Shelley's poem ends. Peter's career was finally crowned twenty years after Shelley's death, when Wordsworth succeeded Southey as Poet Laureate.

Peter Bell the Third was written as a warning against the possible corruption of a great poet by political considerations and self-seeking. Poetry and politics were always intimately related for Shelley. So in other poems we find him warning Byron, too, of those things in his character which might undermine his poetic gift, and therefore his powers for doing good in the world. Shelley had always seen frank assessment of failings as part of friendship: as early as 1813 he wrote to John Williams 'True friendship bears to hear and bears to tell of faults', and Leigh Hunt commented that 'He could both give and take [advice] with an exquisite mixture of frankness and delicacy'. There was criticism of Byron in *Julian and Maddalo* as there is in the fragment:

> O mighty mind in whose deep stream this age
> Shakes like a reed in the unheeding storm
> Why dost thou curb not thine own sacred rage?

Conversely, though Shelley always recognised Byron's flaws, the 1821 sonnet to him shows enormous admiration. Shelley's *Fragment of a Satire on Satire* (1820) reveals both the anger of disappointment and disgust existing in the impulse to satire—'who that has seen/What Southey is and was, would not exclaim/Lash on'—and Shelley's other view, that gentle criticism by a friend may make the erring want to believe in and follow the best in themselves:

> I will only say,
> If any friend would take Southey some day,
> And tell him, in a country walk alone,
> Softening harsh words with friendship's gentle tone,
> How incorrect his public conduct is,
> And what men think of it, 'twere not amiss.   ll. 43–8

This brings us back to a point on which Shelley is always insistent: that political freedom isn't something that can be engineered—hence the danger of revolution. It can come only from within individual men. As he says in his sonnet, *Political Greatness*, 'Man who man would be/Must rule the empire of himself'. Without this Napoleon is no more than Ozymandias. Indeed *Ozymandias*, written the same year as *The Revolt of Islam*, and Shelley's greatest statement on the vanity of human greatness, might serve as a motto for a collection of all his political poems. Beside this sonnet, the *Ode to Liberty*, the *Ode written October 1819 before the Spaniards had recovered their liberty* and the *Ode to Naples* seem long-winded and excessively declamatory. However, these poems do show that Shelley was responsive to the stirrings of liberty in other countries as well as England, though unlike Byron he did not become involved in a practical way. In 1820 there was a revolt in Spain against the Bourbon King Ferdinand VII, restored to the throne after the Napoleonic wars, and this temporarily brought a more liberal government. In Naples a constitutional government set up by rebels was destroyed by the King of Naples with the help of Austria. Of the poems inspired by these events only the *Ode to Liberty* is of much value. In it Shelley traces the growth of liberty from its beginnings in ancient Athens, through its decline in Rome under the influence of a perverted Christianity, to its resurgence through the Reformation and the Bloodless Revolution in England, and to contemporary manifestations in America, Asia and Europe. The poem presents many of Shelley's familiar political ideas, but is perhaps most remarkable for the way the verse takes fire when Shelley talks of Athens (which he never saw). His love for the political and artistic ideals of a society so far distant in time and space is itself inspiring. It is no surprise that he left a number of translations from Plato, Homer and other Greek writers, and wrote original poems on Greek subjects. He had a copy of Sophocles in his pocket when he was drowned.

The pamphlet *A Philosophical View of Reform* was begun at the end of 1819, and covers the same ground as the *Ode to Liberty*, but in systematic and sober fashion, stressing that many past reforms were really compromises. There are impassioned sections—on the role of the poet and philosopher, for instance. If the great men of letters were to speak out against abuses 'it would be like a voice from beyond the dead of those who will live in the memories of men ... it would be Eternity warning time'. Nevertheless the tone is predominantly moderate, as are the opinions. Much of what is advocated—universal suffrage (Shelley envisaged this happening only gradually, and thought Bentham was going too fast in pressing for votes for women), the abolition of sinecures, the introduction of income tax, a reduction of working hours, the elimination of child labour—have become fact, though paper money and the regular army are still with us. Shelley favours peaceful assembly and petitions to demand reforms, backed by passive resistance and non-cooperation including non-payment of taxes. Violent resistance should be only a last resort because of the danger of civil war. Shelley's thinking is all of a piece and it is not surprising to find him including a paragraph from this pamphlet almost word for word in the later *Defence of Poetry* (see Chapter 11).

9

Drama: *The Cenci*; *Charles I*; *Hellas*

Readers of Shelley's other works are unlikely to expect much of him as a playwright. He held his own ideas so passionately, and his attitudes are so consistent, that ventriloquism rather than drama seems the probable outcome of such an attempt. And he recognised his own disqualifications; he thought he was 'too metaphysical and abstract—too fond of the theoretical and the ideal to succeed as a tragedian'. Nevertheless his wife and friends urged him to try his hand and, when a subject which caught his imagination came his way, he wrote rapidly and steadily, completing most of *The Cenci* by July 1819. A year previously Shelley had come across the story of the fall of the Cenci family in an Italian manuscript. When he moved to Rome he found that the story was common currency, and his interest in it was intensified when he visited the ruins of the Cenci palace, and saw a portrait supposedly of Beatrice Cenci attributed to Guido Reni. The picture was to make a deep impression on other writers too —Dickens, Stendhal, Hawthorne. For Shelley, Beatrice Cenci's face was 'one of the loveliest specimens of the workmanship of nature', suggesting a combination of energy and tenderness. Yet she had been executed for the murder of her father. In the story as Shelley found it, the wicked and debauched Count Cenci enjoyed the suffering of others and hated his own children. This prompted an incestuous passion for his daughter Beatrice who, appalled at the contamination, conspired with her stepmother and her brother to kill him. In spite of the extenuating circumstances and appeals to the Pope for clemency the three were put to death.

Shelley took pains with his subject, realising that he was

attempting something quite new for him. 'Those writings which I have hitherto published', he says in his dedication of the play to Leigh Hunt, 'have been little else than visions which impersonate my own apprehensions of the beautiful and the just . . . they are dreams of what ought to be, or may be. The drama which I now present to you is a sad reality.' In a letter he confessed that the dramatic essentials of delineating passion, connecting, and developing it, were for him 'an incredible effort'. For Shelley, then, *The Cenci* was essentially 'a work of art' not coloured by his feelings or obscured by his metaphysics. He claimed not to 'think much of it'. Yet the subject-matter was closer to his basic concerns than Shelley himself admitted: Beatrice, her stepmother and brothers appeal as victims of cruelty and oppression; Beatrice is a tragic figure because, though basically pure and noble, she succumbs to the lure of vengeance; the story gave scope for exposing hypocrisy in the Church; the characters divide into Shelley's usual categories—tyrant, heroic oppressed, priestly time-servers and weak-kneed nonentities. Some of the changes he makes in his source emphasise his habitual attitudes. The Count is turned from an atheist into a practising Catholic whose tyranny is bolstered by the Church's greed for penance payments and by his conviction that he is possessed of near-divine immunity. Threatened by the very existence of his children he feels himself allied to the Pope and to God himself in his assertion of paternal authority. Conversely Beatrice, whose devout prayer before execution is recorded in the source, is more Protestant in attitude, being emphatically keeper of her own conscience, and the appeal she makes to the Pope at the end is not for absolution to ensure forgiveness in the next world, but for life in this. But though the characters are usual Shelleyan types, he showed considerable self-control as well as sustained energy in *The Cenci*. He eliminates obscurity from his style. Speeches are sometimes repetitive to emphasise their emotional content, but the sentences are concise in construction. There are no irrelevant descriptive passages, unless we take exception to the evocation of the ravine where Cenci is to be murdered in Beatrice's first plan, and several contemporary critics thought this the finest poetry of the play. The piece also shows Shelley curbing his natural inclinations. In his previous work the landscape surrounding him makes itself felt. Here, though composed in a sun-baked glass-house with a marvellous view, the work is full of claustrophobic gloom.

Shelley did his best to remove the possible offence of his subject-matter. Incest is referred to only obliquely and, in classical style, all violence takes place off stage. Indeed the play is oddly balanced between the classic and romantic, since it also includes the appeals to emotion of his Elizabethan and Jacobean models. 'Without attaining the repose, dignity and perfect form of classicism', wrote William Archer after witnessing the first performance of the play (not till 1886, and then only a private performance put on by the Shelley Society since it was banned from public performance by the Lord Chamberlain), 'he sacrificed the life, movement, relief, variety of the romantic drama ... *The Cenci* is like the Laocoön group set writhing and roaring for three or four mortal hours by the spell of some wanton magician.' There is justification for Archer's criticism in the excessive use of soliloquy, the long speeches, and the static stage conversations, usually involving only two characters at a time. These sort oddly with emotional appeals to the audience made in Elizabethan style. Hunt the verbal echoes is an all-too-easy game in *The Cenci*. Conscious or unconscious reminiscences of Shakespeare, Webster, Middleton and others abound, and borrowings from *King Lear*, *Macbeth* and *Othello*, in particular, draw attention to their inferiority to the original. Shelley copies admired dramatic situations as well as phrases: he has a banquet ending in 'most admired disorder', given by the Count to celebrate the deaths of his sons, and a trial scene, as in *The White Devil*, in which a guilty woman expresses righteous indignation about the corrupt methods of the court.

When Shelley tried to get the play performed, the manager of Covent Garden Theatre thought the subject-matter too indecent for an actress to read, let alone an audience to pay money to witness. He did, however, detect enough promise in the dramatic construction to ask Shelley to send him a script on any other subject. The very first lines of the play show the economy of the exposition:

> That matter of the murder is hushed up
> If you consent to yield to his Holiness
> Your fief that lies beyond the Pincian gate. I, *i*, 1–3

True, momentum is later lost when Shelley includes scenes which do not forward the action. But he does rise to his climaxes: Beatrice's appeal for help to the assembled guests at the banquet, her speech of shock and horror at having been violated at the beginning of Act III, her father's curse, her trial and the final scene before the execution. As this suggests, Shelley provides two challenging acting parts, those of Cenci and Beatrice. Of the two, Beatrice must be the more difficult; though there are subtleties in the portrayal of the Count, he is at least consistent. His lust for power, his need to stimulate his failing physical capabilities with novelty, his shift from delight in physical torture towards more subtle, mental torment, his self-knowledge, his daring and arrogance are all connected and seem perversions of potentially good qualities such as courage, intellectual clear-sightedness, freedom from remorse. For the first time Shelley produces a tyrant worthy of attention.

Beatrice presents greater problems. Quite apart from the stamina needed—she appears in well over half the scenes of a lengthy play (over four hours at the first performance) and dominates the stage when she is on it—the actress has to try to make sense of what seem inconsistencies in the character. These two factors, Beatrice's pre-eminence when she is on stage and her shifts of behaviour, account for the fact that actresses playing the part have scored personal triumphs while leaving audience and critics in doubt as to Shelley's intention, especially about her motives for denying her guilt, and her apparent indifference to the sufferings of her hired assassins. Alma Murray enormously impressed the audience in the 1886 performance but critics were puzzled that 'instead of avowing the deed, and asserting its justice . . . she tries to avoid death by the meanest arts of false-hood, and encourages her accomplices to endure the extremities of torture rather than implicate her by confession.' Watching Sybil Thorndike play the trial scene in 1922, Shaw realised that he had found the actress for St. Joan, and it may have been Beatrice's youthful longing for life, as well as her courage and her inner certainty of her own innocence, that appealed to him. Certainly, though her speech of horror at the thought of death may look back to *Measure for Measure*, it also looks forward to Joan's recantation of her confession, when she realises that she is to be permanently imprisoned:

> My God! Can it be possible I have
> To die so suddenly? So young to go
> Under the obscure, cold, rotting, wormy ground!
> To be nailed down into a narrow place
> To see no more sweet sunshine.   V, *iv*, 48–52

Barbara Jefford's playing of this collapse impressed *The Times* critic at the 1959 Old Vic production, as did the last speech of the play, which is apt to seem merely derivative to the reader. But clearly the basic problem remained. 'The Lady Macbeth-like creature' who denies complicity at the expense of the tortured assassin is 'strangely unlike the heroine who starts the tragedy for us'. To judge from his Preface, Shelley intends us to think that her character degenerates because of the 'pernicious mistake' of vengeance. But this hardly sorts with the Beatrice of the play, who kills her father mainly to avoid further contamination and to wipe out evil. Her conviction of her own innocence follows naturally from this. If there is a logical connection between this innocence and her determination to survive, even at the expense of others, Shelley doesn't make it plain. Her likeness to her father in such self-preservation may be psychologically probable but offends an audience's notions of poetic justice.

The central action of *The Cenci* is played out against ecclesiastical and court corruption. This is one of the components of the fragment of *Charles I*. In some ways this play shows an advance, both dramatically, in that Shelley makes an attempt to substitute dialogue for near-monologue, and in political attitude, in that we see a little of the complexity of motive that goes to make up the tyrannical king. He is tyrannical because he is weak. His more appealing qualities, such as gratitude for affection and loyalty, subject him to the disproportionate influence of his wife and Strafford, while his sense of being God's representative in England increases Archbishop Laud's power over him. His most decisive actions, giving Strafford supreme authority in Ireland, Laud in Scotland, or the order for the arrest of would-be emigrants to America, are all signs of weakness. In the last case he disregards the wise advice of his Fool, Archy: 'If Your Majesty were tormented night and day by fever, gout, rheumatism and stone and asthma and you found these diseases had secretly entered into a conspiracy to abandon you, should you think it necessary to lay an embargo on the port by which they meant to dispeople your unquiet kingdom of man?' The King makes his decision because he wants to show a kingly courage—'If fear were made for kings, the Fool mocks wisely'. Psychologically he needs to prove himself, because news of the intended rebel voyage was immediately preceded by an argument about whether he should recall Parliament, which hinged on the question of how much the Commons were to be feared.

Predictably it is Archbishop Laud who is the villain of the piece. He may justify torture as an instrument of religious reform, but it is really his instinctive response to threat or criticism. When Bastwick, under sentence of a fine and branding, and imprisonment without term, retains his dignity and exposes the tyranny of the Star Chamber, Laud is all for having his tongue cut out and his hands lopped off. He is restrained only by another judge who points out that it would be bad publicity. His protestation that he shows proper judicial impartiality in sentencing his former benefactor, Bishop Williams, is manifest hypocrisy.

In the fragment we see a number of points of view, from the vigorous criticism of one of the citizens, not untinged with bigotry, to the Fool's poetic truth-telling and wistful song, to Hampden's exalted vision of America. We see Queen Henrietta Maria in more than one light: a Jezebel in the citizens' eyes, a tactless and potentially dangerous queen in St. John's, an affectionate wife and mother, with an interest in the arts, in her private life. Unfortunately the virtues which can be discerned in the fragment do not add up to much, because nothing happens. Each of the four scenes deals with a more or less distinct group of characters, though Laud figures prominently in two. A variety of viewpoint is no substitute for action. The play's desultory beginning makes plain the lack of dramatic impulse that led Shelley to abandon it.

Though there are promising aspects in both *The Cenci* and *Charles I*, neither venture gives real assurance that Shelley would have developed as a dramatist. What can be said, however, is that these experiments might have helped his non-dramatic writings. In style he had to learn economy. More importantly, the effort of trying to present the thoughts of other people led him away from the simplistic attitudes that so seriously mar *Queen Mab* and *The Revolt of Islam*. In theory he had always thought that good and evil were inextricably mingled in human life, but it was only the discipline of drama that led him to realise this in his presentation of individuals.

Even *Hellas* (1821), though it was written in a burst of partisan enthusiasm when a friend, Prince Alexander Mavrocordato, returned to Greece as one of the main leaders of an uprising against the Turks, shows some amiable qualities in the oppressor. Mahmud doesn't really want violence, and feels trapped in the historical process. However, *Hellas* is included in this chapter only for the sake of convenience. Shelley may call it a lyric drama, and may tell us that it is modelled on the *Persae* of Aeschylus, in which news of the battle of Salamis is brought by a messenger to Susa; but even four messengers hot-foot with ill tidings can't disguise the fact that there is no real action. Indeed, it was very difficult for Shelley to provide any, for he had only sketchy information about the events on which *Hellas* was based, and in any case the struggle was only just beginning. The decisive battle, Navarino, came six years later, after Shelley was dead. Though believing in the ultimate triumph of freedom, he was not optimistic about the immediate outcome. He did not expect either Russia or Britain to side with the Greeks. Britain, 'slave and tyrant', would from fear league with the oppressor, and

Russia would watch for eventual advantage from the side-lines.

In the event both supported Greece. So in the drama, if, as he said, 'drama it must be called', he shows long-term hopefulness about the resurgence of Greece, but also short-term depression, since the action ends with news of a Turkish victory. The hopeful signs consist of the four reverses suffered by the Turks, and the inspiring courage of individual rebels in defeat. Furthermore, Mahmud is full of misgivings, especially after he has recalled a doom-laden dream. Once more Ahasuerus, the Wandering Jew, is conveniently resurrected to hypnotise Mahmud into raising the dream-phantom of Mahomet the Second, who prophesies the downfall of his empire. So while Shelley's sympathies are clearly with the Greeks, we see what action there is from the Turkish point of view, additional proof of the growing flexibility of his attitudes. Indeed, one image draws Mahmud quite close to Prometheus in his consciousness of the inevitability of the historical process, though he can feel none of Prometheus's hope for the future:

> Come what may
> The Future must become the Past, and I
> As they were to whom once this present hour,
> This gloomy crag of time to which I cling
> Seemed an Elysian isle of peace and joy
> Never to be attained. ll. 923–8

In fact the most assured verse of *Hellas* is concerned with the inevitability of the resurgence of Greece, especially in the last chorus:

> The world's great age begins anew,
>   The golden years return,
> The earth doth like a snake renew
>   Her winter weeds outworn:
> Heaven smiles, and faiths and empires gleam,
> Like wrecks of a dissolving dream.
>
> A brighter Hellas rears its mountains
>   From waves serener far;
> A new Peneus rolls his fountains
>   Against the morning star. ll. 1060–9

Elsewhere, though there are some vigorous battle reports, Shelley is self-indulgent, a sign of hasty composition. Though he can produce individual arresting lines such as 'And day peers forth with her blank eyes', similes drawn from sky and weather draw attention to themselves rather than clarify the topic in hand. Again he lapses into Shakespearian pastiche. His old fault of ambiguity in the use of pronouns mars the hymn-like chorus beginning 'Worlds on worlds are rolling ever'. Rhymes often seem facile or clumsy. All in all, though his wife thought *Hellas* one of his most beautiful compositions, and though two of the lyrics in particular have been much admired and anthologised, most readers will agree with Shelley himself that it is 'a sort of lyrical, dramatic, nondescript sort of business'. It is, nevertheless, a mark of his veneration for Ancient Greece and his enthusiasm for movements for liberty in his own day, of his love of an ideal and his friendship for an individual. The relationship between his love for the ideal and his love for individuals is the subject of the next chapter.

10

Poems of Love and Friendship

'He was a rock to which limpets stuck fast and periwinkles attached themselves.' 'I never knew anyone so prone to admire as he was, in whom the principle of veneration was so strong.' These two comments by Hogg suggest the two-way traffic of Shelley's friendships. The long poems to be discussed in this chapter, *Letter to Maria Gisborne* and *Epipsychidion*, suggest the range of their intensity. The former, addressed to a much older friend and including a whole family in its reference, is relaxed, easy and playful. The latter, addressed to a young girl, is extravagant, passionate and exclusive, so that it is small wonder that Mary Shelley disliked the poem, referring to it disparagingly as Shelley's 'Italian Platonics'.

Hogg's remark about limpets and periwinkles refers to the way Shelley was exploited financially by others, particularly during his life in England. But the same point is made by Trelawny, who knew him only at the end of his life, when he claims that the Hunts, Peacocks and Godwins 'all sucked his blood'. Shelley was clearly extremely generous financially, sometimes culpably so. But he was not only a financial 'rock'—admittedly of doubtful foundation—but, despite his reputation for changeability, an emotional one. He inspired immediate and lifelong devotion. Nor was this merely the effect of his almost hypnotic charm. He earned devotion by tact and patience also. He looked after Claire and Allegra's interests faithfully without antagonising Byron. Indeed, Byron actually enlisted Shelley's help in dissuading his Italian mistress, Teresa Guiccioli, from going to Switzerland, though Shelley had not even met her. And it was Shelley who organised Byron's removal in 1821 from Ravenna to Pisa, where she was to meet him. This involved renting a palace large enough for a household including a considerable menagerie: Byron had ten horses, eight enormous dogs, three monkeys, five cats, an eagle, a crow and a falcon, all, horses excepted, having the free run of the house. Shelley adds a post-script to a letter to Peacock revealing whimsical enjoyment of his friend's idiosyncrasy: 'I find my enumeration of the animals in this Circean Palace was defective, and that in a material point. I have just met on the grand staircase five peacocks, two guinea hens, and an Egyptian crane. I wonder who all these animals were before they were changed into these shapes.' However, though Byron was stimulating company and had, under Teresa's influence, settled after a period of dissipation, Shelley could not entirely approve of him, and wanted to detach himself.

Meanwhile tact was needed in keeping Claire out of the way, and also in preparing Byron for the arrival from England of Leigh Hunt and his family. Shelley hoped that Byron would give Hunt support in setting up a new periodical to be called 'The Liberal', and the Hunt family were to live in part of Byron's house. Shelley helped Hunt with money for the journey. He had also set about finding a house for one of his most faithful friends, Horace Smith, who, however, never arrived because his wife fell ill in Paris.

Previously others had benefited from Shelley's hospitality. His cousin, Tom Medwin, had come to Pisa in October 1820, and Shelley had nursed him through a six weeks' illness, though he was ill himself. Medwin introduced new friends, Edward and Jane Williams, and Trelawny. In fact Shelley had more friends near him in the last two years of his life than ever before. He seems to have been the centre of this rather diverse circle; certainly after his death it quickly split up, though individual members of it were constant in their admiration of Shelley to the end of their lives—almost sixty years later Trelawny was buried next to Shelley in Rome.

Shelley is often at his most engaging when least intense, as in his letters, or in the verse epistle to Maria Gisborne. The Gisbornes were the Shelleys' first friends in Italy. Mrs. Gisborne had known Mary as a baby, and when widowed had refused a proposal of marriage from Godwin, marrying John Gisborne instead. The warmth of the friendship varied. At first Shelley thought John Gisborne boring, but he later wrote him intimate and interesting letters, and used him to negotiate with Godwin when the Gisbornes finally returned to England in 1821. There was some coolness in late 1820. Mrs. Gisborne's son by her first marriage, Henry Reveley, was an engineer, and this revived Shelley's scientific interests. It also called forth his philanthropic spirit. He helped finance Henry's project for building a steamboat: 'Your boat will be to the ocean of water what the earth is to the ocean of aether—a prosperous and swift voyager.' Hopefully, the voyaging was to be between Marseilles and Leghorn, but in late 1820 the scheme was abandoned, perhaps partly because Shelley had pressed for an unworkably large engine.

Shelley probably lost nearly £400 when the remnants of the boat were sold off, and in the disappointment referred to the Gisbornes as 'totally without faith', though he was the same day writing in friendly style to Gisborne about dictionaries and Arabic grammars. There are, however, no signs of these coming frictions in *Letter to Maria Gisborne*, written in July 1820 when the Gisbornes had gone on a trip to England and the Shelleys were living in their house at Leghorn. In the summer of 1820 there is still the affection, playfulness and intellectual easiness suggested by a letter of October 1819, when Shelley was looking after the Gisbornes' dog: 'His importunate regret is however a type as regards you. Our memory—if you will forgive so humble a metaphor—is forever scratching at the door of your absence.' In the poem Shelley is again scratching at the door of her absence and of his separation from London friends. But the scratching isn't at all desperate, for the poem tells us as much about his enjoyment of Italy as his nostalgia for England.

In the opening lines Shelley, to moralists a mere worm of a poet, compares himself to a spider or silk worm. The poem which follows is itself spun from threads of past, present and future —dead but immortal poets and living friends, poetry and science, landscape and skyscape in England and Italy, outer storms and domestic warmth, nostalgia and hope. This particular web is not being constructed in a poet's tower, but in an engineer's study. Shelley is enjoying sitting at Henry Reveley's desk surrounded by his diagrams and scientific equipment: the 'dead engines' remind him of the mythical devices of Vulcan, the historical 'engines' of the Spanish Inquisition, and references in Shakespeare, Sidney and Spenser. On the study floor are bits and pieces for the steamboat:

> Great screws, and cones, and wheels, and grooved blocks,
> The elements of what will stand the shocks
> Of wave and wind and time.   ll. 52–4

On the desk is another boat—one of Shelley's paper ones, afloat on a bowl of mercury. Gnomes or devils might drink from the walnut bowl, gleeful as Shakespearean fairies, but the dark wood enclosing quicksilver also reminds him of 'The Tuscan deep, when from the moist moon rains/The inmost shower of its white fire'. Mixed up with the nautical charts and steamboat plans is a third vessel, a china teacup: 'A thing from which sweet lips were wont to drink/The liquor doctors rail at—and which I/Will quaff in spite of them.' This suggestion of frugal conviviality recurs at ll. 150–2, and at the end of the poem, with a pleasing picture of Shelley's ascetic gluttony:

> Though we eat little flesh and drink no wine,
> Yet let's be merry: we'll have tea and toast;
> Custards for supper, and an endless host
> Of syllabubs and jellies and mince-pies,
> And other such lady-like luxuries,—
> Feasting on which we will philosophise!   ll. 302–7

Line 106 transforms Shelley from a follower, however mystified, of Archimedes into a Spenserian Archimago, 'plotting dark spells' as he hears the wind, sees the vines tremble and the hill whiten under 'electric rain'. Coleridge's 'Frost at Midnight', which Shelley echoes at l. 123, uses weather as a pivot for memory and hope, for thoughts of London and the country. Shelley's poem follows a similar pattern. This storm reminds him of watching one with Maria Gisborne, while indoors the empty chairs recall their former occupants. Mrs. Gisborne had taught him Spanish (as before he had learnt Italian with the Boinvilles). Now she is in London seeing friends. Tersely and discerningly Shelley describes them. Though Godwin caused him pain and disappointment, Shelley still gives honour where honour is due:

> You will see
> That which was Godwin,—greater none than he
> Though fallen—and fallen on evil times—to stand
> Among the spirits of our age and land,
> Before the dread tribunal of *to come*
> The foremost,—while Rebuke cowers pale and dumb.
>
> ll. 197–201

Coleridge's immense potential and marred achievement are sympathetically caught:

> You will see Coleridge—he who sits obscure
> In the exceeding lustre and the pure
> Intense irradiation of a mind,
> Which, with its own internal lightning blind,
> Flags wearily through darkness and despair—
> A cloud-encircling meteor of the air,
> A hooded eagle among blinking owls.
>
> ll. 202–8

Portraits of Hunt, Hogg and Peacock all show enjoyment of the personality each presents to the world, and an understanding of the beings that lie behind. The aesthete Hunt, who had even his prison cell papered with wreaths of flowers, is actually 'the salt of the earth'; Hogg uses his wit to 'barricade' his virtues; Peacock's wit 'makes such a wound, the knife is lost in it'. The most straightforward praise is accorded not to the better known writers but to the stockbroker, Horace Smith, who combines 'wit and sense, virtue and human knowledge'. ('Is it not odd', Shelley commented to Hunt, 'that the only truly generous person I ever knew, who had money to be generous with, should be a stockbroker?').

In the last paragraph Shelley turns from thoughts of London—

like Coleridge it was in the sky that he found beauty above the squalor of the city—to hopes for friendly reunions in Italy. He did see the Gisbornes again when they came back to wind up their affairs. And it was on the way home from meeting the Hunts at Leghorn that Shelley was drowned. But, Byron and Medwin apart, it was mainly among new friends that Shelley spent the last eighteen months of his life.

The most intense of these friendships—and the briefest—was with the nineteen-year-old Emilia Viviani, the inspiration of *Epipsychidion*. She appealed as another victim of 'oppression', having been immured in a convent until such time as an economically suitable husband could be found for her. Mary and Shelley visited her frequently in December 1820 and the early months of 1821. In September she married. Having made a great impression on Shelley by her beauty, intelligence and literary aspirations (she had already written poems and a rhapsody on Love) she now disappointed him by her acquiescence in the match that had been arranged for her, completing the disillusionment by a request for a large loan.

Epipsychidion was written in February 1821. Enthusiasm had cooled by the time of its publication in the summer. In his Advertisement to the poem Shelley maintains the fiction that it is the work of a dead friend. In part this is to put a safe distance between its autobiographical content and curious and hostile critics. But it also reflects the death of Shelley's admiration for Emilia, and his sense of isolation. 'It is a production of a portion of me already dead.' Two letters of 22 October reveal this attitude. To the cynical Hogg he wrote: 'I . . . live in a total intellectual solitude. I knew a very interesting Italian lady last winter but she is now married; which to quote our friend Peacock, is you know the same as being dead.' To John Gisborne he said: 'Some of us have in a prior existence been in love with an Antigone, and that makes us find no full content in any mortal tie.' Eight months later he told him that he could not look at the poem because 'the person it celebrates was a cloud instead of a Juno'. The *Hymn of Pan* of 1820 suggests that such disappointment was not new to Shelley:

> down the vale of Maenalus
> I pursued a maiden and clasped a reed.
> Gods and men we are all deluded thus!
> It breaks in our bosom and then we bleed.   ll. 30–3

Seven years after writing *Alastor*, Shelley's problem was still the same. The veiled maiden still eluded him: 'I think one is always in love with something or other; the error, and I confess it is not easy for spirits cased in flesh and blood to avoid it, consists in seeking in a mortal image the likeness of what is perhaps eternal.'

Shelley himself said that the *Epipsychidion* is a mystery. The title is deliberately rarefied. The word, formed by analogy with 'epicycle' (a small circle revolving on the circumference of a larger one), suggests the complementariness of two souls or psyches, and Shelley's dependence on the ideal of Emilia—the 'embodied Ray/Of the great Brightness'. There are other mystifications in the poem. It is 'an idealised history' of his life and feelings, and it is clear that Mary is represented by the Moon and Emilia by the Sun; but the identification of the 'One whose voice was venomed melody' (l. 256) or the Comet (l. 368) is perplexing.

Though the gist of the poem is clear, details are obscure. Shelley's irritating addiction to negative prefixes and suffixes seems the result either of carelessness—the whole poem sounds a breathless improvisation—or a deliberate attempt to remove love from the sexual to a more ethereal plane, sometimes baffling the reader in the process. Though there are authoritatively simple lines such as 'I am not thine; I am a part of *thee*', or 'The spirit of the worm beneath the sod/In love and worship, blends itself with God', adoration of Emilia is expressed in such a rapid succession of images that the reader is apt to need the reassurance of Shelley's self-criticism:

> I measure
> The world of fancies, seeking one like thee,
> And find—alas! mine own infirmity.   ll. 69–71

Even the opening, where one hopes for guidance, is oblique:

> Sweet Spirit! Sister of that orphan one,
> Whose empire is the name thou weepest on,
> In my heart's temple I suspend to thee
> These votive wreaths of withered memory.   ll. 1-4

He longs to be able to harmonise his love for this new sweet spirit with his love for his wife, 'orphan' of Mary Wollstencraft. Later they hold sway over him as sun and moon, one of the main arguments of the poem being that love should not be exclusive, that diversity in love does not mean diminution but rather enrichment. There is room for sisters and spouses. Still Shelley does get confused between them and a part of him longs for a passionate, exclusive relationship represented by the beautiful idyll beginning at l. 407 in which he dreams of sailing away with Emilia to a Greek island paradise, itself 'an atom of the Eternal'. The love will be spiritual—the 'passion in twin-hearts' recalls his hankering in l. 45 to be Emilia's twin brother—but Shelley looks forward to a physical expression of it:

> Our breath shall intermix, our bosoms bound,
> And our veins beat together.   ll. 565-6

Mary, who is cast in the somewhat chilly role of moon-goddess in this poem, had the satisfaction of receiving a letter written after the publication of *Epipsychidion* but before Emilia married, in which Shelley once more expresses a longing to escape to an island solitude: 'My greatest content would be utterly to desert all human society. I would retire with you and our child to a solitary island in the sea . . . love far more than hatred has been to me, except as you have been its object, the source of all sorts of mischief.'

In *Epipsychidion*, however, Emilia is pre-eminent. From being a pitiable captive bird in l. 5, she sprouts seraphic wings by l. 21, to become light itself: moon at l. 26, star, a mirror of the sun, a lamp drawing Shelley's moth-like soul. As in *Alastor* there is some doubt as to whether this attraction is life-giving or death-bringing. The analogies (ll. 72-5) are confusing—she 'lured' him 'towards sweet Death', but 'led into light, life, peace'. Perhaps this is only another way of saying that Shelley could not believe that the appearances of life were the ultimate reality. Though such

mixed emotions may give rise to striking metaphors and similes
such as:

> in the soul a wild odour is felt
> Beyond the sense, like fiery dews that melt
> Into the bosom of a frozen bud.   ll. 109–11

or 'A Metaphor of Spring and Youth and Morning', in real life
they tend to lead to a distressing confusion of roles. To be
'Spouse! Sister! Angel! Pilot of the Fate/Whose course has been
so starless' (ll. 130–2) is too much to ask of one inexperienced girl.
And one might object that the trouble with Shelley was not that
he lacked stars, but that he came across too many, some of his
own creating. The bridge between the first section of praise
for Emilia, and a veiled account of his past experiences, is a
passage justifying diversity in love. 'Love is like understanding,
that grows bright/Gazing on many truths', and like imagination,
flaking off light from prisms and mirrors:

> Narrow
> The heart that loves, the brain that contemplates,
> The life that wears, the spirit that creates
> One object, and one form.   ll. 169–73

Here we have Shelley trying to dismiss his yearning for oneness in favour of his attraction to the multiform. These two op-
posing and strongly felt impulses, noted in earlier poems, are
more successfully adjusted in the other extended poem of praise
which Shelley wrote in the early summer of 1821, *Adonais* (see
Chapter 11). There he has a more satisfactory 'star': John Keats.
He could suffer no disillusionment with him, because Keats, who
in life avoided intimacy with Shelley, was removed by death;
besides, the ideal was not in this case complicated by sex. But in
Epipsychidion, when, after an *Alastor*-like prevision of the ideal
(ll. 190–215), Shelley tells of his encounters with potential
embodiments of it, the attempt smacks of self-pity ('And one
was true—oh! why not true to me') or guilty self-justification
('from her living cheeks and bosom flew/A killing air, which
pierced like honey-dew/Into the core of my green heart').

It is rather a relief to turn from Shelley's endeavour to reconcile the conflicting claims of the women in his life to frank daydreaming in the last section of the poem. The couplets assume a supple grace as Shelley evokes a *Tempest*-like island of sandy beaches and 'sweet airs'. Here external nature and two individual souls, dream and reality, are all in harmony:

> And every motion, odour, beam and tone,
> With that deep music is in unison:
> Which is a soul within the soul—they seem
> Like echoes of an antenatal dream. ll. 453–6

Hints of *The Tempest* form a link with the poems addressed to Jane Williams in 1822. Encouraged by Tom Medwin, whom they had known in India, Edward and Jane Williams came to Pisa in the spring of 1821 to meet Shelley. Edward was a half-pay lieutenant in the East India Company Army, but he had also been in the Navy. Jane was his common-law wife, having been deserted by her husband. In June 1821 Shelley described them, possibly reflecting disillusionment with Emilia, as 'nice, good-natured people; very soft society after authors and pretenders to philosophy'. Actually Williams had literary aspirations, as had Medwin and their friend Trelawny who joined the Pisan circle in January 1822. But Shelley valued Williams particularly as a boating companion. The pleasure (complete with flask of tea) of sailing their skiff is recaptured in 'The Boat on the Serchio'. To Williams he confided a feeling that Mary was cold and aloof towards him. In the poem beginning 'The serpent is shut out from Paradise' once again Shelley reveals a craving for pity; longing for home easily becomes longing for death:

> The crane o'er seas and forests seeks her home;
> No bird so wild but has its quiet nest,
> When it no more would roam;
> The sleepless billows on the ocean's breast
> Break like a bursting heart, and die in foam,
> And thus at length find rest:
> Doubtless there is a place of peace
> Where *my* weak heart and all its throbs will cease. ll. 41–8

Increasingly the love of friends and mutability are entwined as themes in his lyrics. Isolated moments of pleasure are poignantly enhanced by recognition of their evanescence. This gives memorable intensity to straightforward description in 'Evening: Ponte al Mare, Pisa' and a tough delicacy to 'Mutability';

> The flower that smiles to-day
> > To-morrow dies;
> All that we wish to stay
> > Tempts and then flies.
> What is this world's delight?
> Lightning that mocks the night,
> > Brief even as bright.
>
> Virtue, how frail it is!
> > Friendship how rare!
> Love, how it sells poor bliss
> > For proud despair!
> But we, though soon they fall,
> Survive their joy, and all
> > Which ours we call.   ll. 1–14

Shelley had liked Ned Williams immediately, but admiration for Jane came slowly. Gradually he found her placidity soothing, till in January 1822 he referred to her as 'a sort of spirit of embodied peace in our circle of tempests'. She had two accomplishments that endeared her. She was able to give Shelley some relief from the nerve pains that afflicted him, by hypnotism, and she sang well. In 'The Magnetic Lady to her Patient' he imagines her words of pity but acknowledges that she does not and cannot love him. Using characters from *The Tempest* Shelley suggests the tenderness and the limits of their relationship while he praises her musical skill in *With a Guitar, to Jane*. The guitar is Ariel's gift to Miranda 'by permission and command/Of thine own Prince Ferdinand'. So Shelley can gracefully assure Jane of his love and admiration without intruding on her exclusive relationship with Williams. Shelley's present is 'a silent token/Of more than ever can be spoken' in two senses—the emotion is inexpressible because intense, and because it demands restraint. The guitar needs Jane to awaken its melody, like memories of the wind in the Italian pine tree from which it was made. The last four lines combine urbane compliment for Jane's musical skill, veneration for her ability to inspire, and familiar affection:

> But sweetly as its answers will
> Flatter hands of perfect skill,
> It keeps its highest, holiest tone
> For our beloved Jane alone.   ll. 87–90

Here the regularity of the well-tried form (octosyllabic couplets) maintains the balance between seriousness and whimsicality. But for brief intensity he invents his own verse forms. 'Music when soft voices die', 'Mutability', 'O world! O life, O time', 'When the lamp is shattered', 'The keen stars are twinkling' and 'We meet not as we parted' share an intensity of longing and regret but are very varied in form. Indeed, the interplay between rhyme and metre becomes increasingly subtle towards the end of Shelley's life. He produces forms each of which seems to be the natural medium for what he has to say. In fact they arise not only from past experimentation but also from past discipline, failures included, in following established and demanding forms such as the Spenserian stanza.

This apparently instinctive choice of rhyme/metre combination according to subject and mood can be seen in two companion poems to Jane. *The Invitation* calls her outside to enjoy a morning of early spring in the Italian countryside. The couplets suggest haste and eagerness, but Shelley avoids the sing-song by his variation of seven, eight and occasional nine-syllabled lines. He can as easily adopt a cavalier attitude—'Today is for itself enough', as a Wordsworthian one—'While the touch of Nature's art/Harmonises heart to heart', and can suggest more than he says by the final rallentando:

> And the blue noon is over us,
> And the multitudinous
> Billows murmur at our feet,
> Where the earth and ocean meet,
> And all things seem only one
> In the universal sun.   ll. 64–9

The Recollection avoids the insistence of couplets, settling, after an introductory stanza, into alternate rhymes, suiting the meditative mood. Jane's soothing presence and the beauty of nature harmonise to provide for Shelley a rare moment of calm, binding 'our mortal nature's strife' to 'momentary peace'. Gratitude for the moment and regret for its passing are fused. No wonder Shelley was attracted to 'immovably unquiet' images in water when they so accurately reflected his own nature:

> Less oft is peace in Shelley's mind,
> Than calm in waters seen.   ll. 87–8

Self-criticism salts self-pity in *Lines Written in the Bay of Lerici*. The poem recaptures the stillness and beauty of evening merging into night when Jane has left him gazing at the bay, a beauty which nevertheless includes death and pain:

> And the fisher with his lamp
> And spear about the low rocks damp
> Crept, and struck the fish which came
> To worship the delusive flame.   ll. 45–8

Shelley draws one moral from the episode:

> Too happy they, whose pleasure sought
> Extinguishes all sense and thought
> Of the regret that pleasure leaves,
> Destroying life alone, not peace!   ll. 49–52

But he leaves us to pursue the fish/Shelley analogy for ourselves. This variation, in one of Shelley's last poems, of the moth/star attraction may assure us that, had he lived, Shelley's preoccupations were likely to remain much the same, but that toughness could underpin the lyric grace.

11

Defending Poets and Poetry

Two events early in 1821 turned Shelley's mind to the defence of
poets and poetry: his perusal of Peacock's *The Four Ages of
Poetry*, published in Ollier's *Literary Miscellany*, and news, reaching
him in April, of Keats's death. In his essay Peacock had divided
the history of poetry into four phases: the iron when 'rude bards
celebrate in rough numbers, the exploits of ruder chiefs'; the
golden, in which poetry reaches perfection, as yet unchallenged
by history, science and philosophy; the silver, in which poetry
becomes over-refined; and the brass, a pseudo-golden age in
which poets actually return to barbarism. English poetry, having
passed through the ages of Chaucer, Shakespeare, and Dryden
and Pope, had now arrived at its brass age, and the poet was
now 'a semi-barbarian in a civilised community'. This partly
playful onslaught excited Shelley to 'sacred rage'. As he wrote to
Peacock: 'I had the greatest possible desire to break a lance with
you . . . in honour of my mistress Urania.' Meanwhile Keats was
dying of consumption, his health undermined, Shelley thought,
by the distress caused by a hostile notice of *Endymion* in the
Quarterly Review, a magazine which had also criticised Shelley.
He therefore had a personal motive, too, for wanting to defend
poetry in general and individual poets in particular.

Shelley never wrote the second and third parts of the *Defence
of Poetry* in which he planned to examine and defend contemporary poetry; in the first part, not published till 1840, most direct
references to *The Four Ages of Poetry* were eliminated. But Peacock's essay provokes the historical survey in the *Defence*, and
its insistence on poetry's universality and moral usefulness. The
first section of the *Defence* concentrates on poetry as the greatest

expression of the imagination. Whereas reason is the faculty of analysis and perceives differences, imagination is the faculty of synthesis and of perceiving similitudes. 'Reason is to imagination as the instrument to the agent, as the body to the spirit, as the shadow to the substance.' This series of analogies implies, characteristically for Shelley, that spirit is more 'substantial' than body, an idea recurring in *Adonais*. Here the insistence on imagination as an evaluating faculty prepares us for sections later on in which it is seen as 'the great instrument of moral good', particularly necessary in the modern world. Intervening, however, is Shelley's discussion of the place of poetry as 'the expression of the imagination' from the beginnings of human society. The first philosophers, instituters of law, teachers, founders of religion were all poets in the broadest sense. 'Poets . . . were called in the earlier epochs of the world legislators and prophets; a poet essentially comprises and unites both these characters.' A poet 'participates in the eternal, the infinite and the one; as far as relates to his conceptions, time and place and number are not'.

It is because this universality is the prime essential of poetry that Shelley refuses to separate verse and prose rigidly; Plato and Bacon are both poets in his eyes. It was on these grounds that Sidney, too, had defended poetry against Plato's criticism of its lack of 'truth'. Plato was suspicious of the pleasures of poetry —they were likely to be delusive. But for Shelley the pleasure of poetry is the basis of its moral usefulness, not merely in the sense that it sugars a pill of didacticism. Rather, 'it awakens and enlarges the mind itself by rendering it the receptacle of a thousand unapprehended combinations of thought. Poetry lifts the veil from the hidden beauty of the world . . . The great secret of morals is love, or a going out of our own nature and an identification of ourselves with the beautiful which exists in thought, action, or person, not our own. A man, to be greatly good, must imagine intensely and comprehensively; he must put himself in the place of another and of many others; the pains and pleasures of his species must become his own'. These ideas are already familiar from the Preface to *The Revolt of Islam*. It is because poetry makes for moral good indirectly, by teaching us to love the beautiful, that explicitly didactic poetry can never be the most valuable.

Shelley goes on to prove his points by a survey of poetry from Homer to the present day. Naturally enough he follows the pattern of his history of political freedom in the *Ode to Liberty* and *A Philosophical View of Reform*, since it is one of his tenets that the great ages of literature are ages of political advance. His discussion of drama is governed by his belief in universality as poetry's essential quality, as well as in the enlarging of the imagination as a moral good. For instance, he is attracted to the ancient practice of the actor's wearing a mask 'on which the many expressions appropriate to his dramatic character might be moulded into one permanent and unchanging expression'. Again, rightly handled, as in *King Lear*, the blending of comedy with tragedy adds to the universality, and Shelley believes Shakespeare's play to be 'the most perfect specimen of the dramatic art existing in the world'. Shelley attempts to account for the beneficial effect of the tragic pleasures of 'pity, indignation, terror and sorrow'. They induce an 'exalted calm'. Furthermore tragedy shows crime arising from 'the unfathomable agencies of nature', not from man's wilfulness. So, he asserts, 'In a drama of the highest order there is little food for censure or hatred; it teaches rather self-knowledge and self-respect'. This accords with Shelley's insistence in *The Revolt of Islam*, *Prometheus Unbound* and elsewhere that men need to think well of themselves before they can act well, and that self-contempt and hatred of others are closely allied. In passing, it is arguable that an examination of the character of Edmund in *King Lear* would endorse this view.

At its best, drama enlarges men's sympathies, but not all drama is imaginative. In the period of Charles II tragedies affected 'sentiment and passion which, divested of imagination, are other names for caprice and appetite'. All becomes mere calculation. 'Comedy loses its ideal universality; wit succeeds to humour; we laugh from self-complacency and triumph, instead of pleasure.' Similar ups and downs are discernible in other forms of poetry. Pastoral and erotic poetry may be imperfect because of exclusive concentration on one sentiment, for what is lacking rather than what is included. But Shelley sees even lesser poetic productions as 'episodes to that great poem to which all poets, like the co-operating thoughts of one great mind, have built up since the beginning of the world'. This notion of the comradeship of all poets, irrespective of the time in which they lived, is voiced in *Adonais*. It is in keeping with Shelley's by now familiar dual love of oneness and of the multiform, which finds its final expression in the elegy on Keats. One of poetry's most important functions is to find harmony in this duality: poetry 'marries exultation and horror, grief and pleasure, eternity and change; it subdues to union, under its light yoke, all irreconcilable things . . . its secret alchemy turns to potable gold the poisonous waters which flow from death through life.' *Adonais* bears this out.

There has been a good deal of discussion as to whether in the final stanzas of *Adonais* Shelley is expressing a death wish, or is aspiring to new poetic life. On the evidence of the *Defence* either view seems too simple. True, he flirted with suicide; not long before he died he was requesting prussic acid from Trelawny. But he also believed that 'Poetry is the record of the best and happiest moments of the happiest and best minds'. Certainly pain is involved in the poetic process because 'the mind in creation is as a fading coal which an inconstant wind awakens to transitory brightness'; and even 'the most glorious poetry . . . is probably a feeble shadow of the original conceptions of the poet'. Nevertheless there is also pleasure, even in the 'desire and regret' left by evanescent experiences, since the mind participates in 'the nature of its object'. So 'poetry redeems from decay the visitations of the divinity in man'.

Shelley insists on the intuitive nature of poetry. This is the secret of its moral benefit. After all it is not 'for want of admirable doctrines that men hate, and despise and censure, and deceive, and subjugate one another'. It is for want of imagination. Though Shelley was in favour of scientific exploration and experimentation he did not believe that knowledge was enough :'We want [i.e. lack] the creative faculty to imagine that which we know . . . man, having enslaved the elements, remains himself a slave.'

Beholding 'the future in the present', Shelley remains a prophet for our own times.

Keats and Shelley had known each other through Leigh Hunt. From the beginning Shelley admired Keats though he did not refrain from criticism. Keats, more wary, declined to visit Shelley that he might retain his own 'unfettered scope'. Hearing of Keats's illness in July 1820, Shelley invited him to Pisa: 'This consumption is a disease particularly fond of people who write such good verses as you have done, and with the assistance of an English winter it can often indulge its selection; I do not think that young and amiable poets are at all bound to gratify its taste; they have entered into no bond with the Muses to that effect.' When he learned that Keats had arrived in Italy with Joseph Severn, Shelley still hoped to be useful to him, though he said he would be 'nourishing a rival' who would 'far surpass' him. But Keats went first to Naples and then to Rome where he died on 23 February, 1821. He was buried in the Protestant cemetery. Shelley knew the place well, since his son had been buried there. An open space among the ruins of the walls of ancient Rome, it was, Shelley tells us, covered in winter with violets and daisies: 'It might make one in love with death, to think one should be buried in so sweet a place.' Within two years his own ashes were interred there.

Shelley did not know all the harrowing circumstances of Keats's death when he wrote *Adonais*. If he had, he would not, he thought, have been able to finish it, he would have felt too closely involved. As it was, his belief that Keats was struck down as a direct result of the attack in the *Quarterly*, combined with his resentment at its treatment of *The Revolt of Islam*, provided one of the motive forces of the poem. Shelley may have been able to shrug off the attacks—he makes fun of them with considerable verve in a letter to Maria Gisborne—but he was disheartened by lack of recognition. Even so, the literary magazines were on the whole kinder to Shelley than to Keats. Perhaps overestimating Keats's vulnerability, and increasingly convinced that he was 'a great genius', Shelley was anxious to defend him. He recognised the enormous advance on *Endymion* represented by

Keats's 1820 volume, particularly valuing *Hyperion*. A copy of this volume was found in his pocket after he drowned, doubled back as if he had just been reading it and had hastily thrust it away. So equally important motives for *Adonais* were veneration for Keats, and grief at the loss of his youth and potential.

Adonais is a pastoral elegy, taking as its models particularly an elegy on Adonis attributed to Bion (Shelley left a translation of some of this) and an elegy on Bion attributed to Moschus (both Greek poets of the second century B.C.). Like Milton's *Lycidas*, its English forerunner, Shelley's poem has been criticised for not telling us enough about the person mourned, and for including sections that are too self-concerned (ll. 108–31 of *Lycidas* in which Milton gives us his views on the clergy, and ll. 271–306 of *Adonais* in which Shelley himself appears). Though he knew Keats better than Milton knew Edward King, Shelley over-exaggerated the effect of criticism on Keats, and under-estimated the toughness of his character. However there are more indications of Shelley's love and understanding of Keats's poetry than might at first appear. He chose a form in which references to and echoes of Keats's writing could be seamlessly incorporated. Both poets were drawn to the music of the Spenserian stanza, realising its potential for narrative and for picture painting. Both *The Eve of St. Agnes* and *Adonais* combine a statuesque quality in description with an underlying preoccupation with flux and change. *Adonais* is more explicit and less unified; for one thing Shelley is writing elegy not narrative, for another he is essentially a poet of ideas, Keats of sensation. Of course this bald statement over-simplifies, since each was seeking to modify his natural inclination with its opposite: Keats to deal with intellectual problems, Shelley to become more detached from his pet ideas. In the greatest work of each, thought and emotion or sensation are so fused that categorisation becomes meaningless. As Shelley says in the *Defence*, 'all high poetry is infinite; it is as the first acorn, which contained all oaks potentially. Veil after veil may be withdrawn and the inmost naked beauty of the meaning never exposed'.

Keats is reflected in *Adonais* not only in the choice and handling of verse form, and in echoes or references to his poems, for example the hint of *Isabella* at ll. 48 and 172, or the nightingale at l. 145, or to the epic strain of *Hyperion* at l. 148. Shelley's poetic representation of Keats's characteristic subject-matter and method from l. 100 onwards is precise and just. It fits with the pastoral and with Shelley's own style, but it is peculiarly applicable to Keats rather than to any other English poet. The first point is that Keats largely by-passes the cerebral, entrancing with richness of physical detail and verbal music; one of his splendours is:

> strength to pierce the guarded wit,
> And pass into the panting heart beneath
> With lightning and with music.   ll. 102–4

This accords with Keats's own exclamation, 'O for a life of sensations rather than of thoughts', and also his advice to Shelley to 'load every rift of your subject with ore'. What may at first seem a Shelleyan procession of abstractions in the next stanza in fact also calls to mind the withdrawing dreams of *Endymion*, the aspirations of *Hyperion*, the darkling world of the *Ode to a Nightingale*, the mists of Autumn and the apprehension of mingled pain and pleasure most explicit in the *Ode on Melancholy*, but underlying all Keats's late poems. In 'Pleasure blind with tears' Shelley adroitly echoes Keats's 'aching pleasure', while allowing her embodiment as a mourner in his poem:

> And others came . . . Desires and Adorations,
> Winged Persuasions and veiled Destinies,
> Splendours, and Glooms, and glimmering Incarnations
> Of hopes and fears, and twilight Phantasies;
> And Sorrow and her family of Sighs,
> And Pleasure, blind with tears, led by the gleam
> Of her own dying smile instead of eyes,
> Came in slow pomp;—the moving pomp might seem
> Like pageantry of mist on an autumnal stream.   ll. 109–17

Shelley sums up concisely Keats's essential quality as a poet in his expression of grief:

> All he had loved and moulded into thought
> From shape, and hue, and odour, and sweet sound
> Lamented *Adonais*.   ll. 118–20

Keats's raw materials are shapes, colours, scents and sounds. Through the processes of imaginative synthesis which Shelley discussed in the *Defence*, he 'moulded them into thought'. His greatest work married 'exultation and horror, grief and pleasure, eternity and change'.

This, too, is the prime purpose of an elegy. In *Adonais* Shelley follows the traditional pattern. Mourners lament the young poet, chief among them Urania, goddess of heavenly love, and Milton's Muse, whom he regards as Keats's mother. The formal opening stanzas become, after the characterisation of Keats, immediately personal at l. 154:

> Ah woe is me! Winter is come and gone
> But grief returns with the revolving year.

The grief is all the more poignant when we remember Shelley's usual expectations of spring. Dead bodies may nourish new life but have we any assurance that the spirit endures?

> Great and mean
> Meet massed in death, who lends what life must borrow.
> As long as skies are blue, and fields are green,
> Evening must usher night, night urge the morrow,
> Month follow month with woe, and year wake year to sorrow.
>   ll. 185–9

Amongst the mourners are contemporary poets, Byron (actually rather scornful of Keats), Tom Moore, Shelley himself and Leigh Hunt, the only one to have been a close friend. However, this gathering establishes a poetic quorum for attacking the critics who had 'killed' Keats. Pitying contempt for the 'carrion kites' launches Shelley into an impassioned justification of Keats and affirmation of the spirit of Keats and of poetry. Keats is 'a portion of the Eternal', part of the great creative spirit, the divine energy of love flowing through poetry, nature and all life. Shelley draws together the subdued water images in the poem and the frequent light, flame and fire images when he affirms that 'the pure spirit shall flow/Back to the burning fountain whence it came'. He is united with what Shelley calls 'the one Spirit', but through that 'made one with Nature', and so dispersed into, for example, 'the song of night's sweet bird' which he himself celebrated. Adonais is 'a presence to be felt and known' in the manifestations of time, but he has also escaped its confines. Death is more apparent than real.

Shelley draws together the personal and impersonal as he meditates on the Rome burial ground: 'Like an infant's smile over the dead/A light of laughing flowers along the grass is spread'—the daisies which Shelley remembered and which Keats asked should be allowed to grow over his grave. For a last time Shelley's favourite image for co-existing evanescence and permanence appears: Keats lies near the pyramid of Caius Cestus; though Time feeds on the crumbling walls around 'like slow fire upon a hoary brand', the memorial stands 'Like flame transformed to marble'. So the pathos of individual loss is put in a larger perspective. If, as Blake said, 'Eternity is in love with the productions of time', there is beauty in the world for men to celebrate. But there is also the longing to escape from the fragmentation of space and time. Shelley captures this duality in one of his most marvellous and complex light images:

> From the world's bitter wind
> Seek shelter in the shadow of the tomb.
> What Adonais is why fear we to become?
>
> The One remains, the many change and pass;
> Heaven's light forever shines, Earth's shadows fly;
> Life, like a dome of many-coloured glass,
> Stains the white radiance of Eternity,
> Until Death tramples it to fragments.   ll. 457–64

It seems simple-minded to expect Shelley's meaning to be less prismatic than his imagery. So the last two stanzas of the poem can be read either as a longing for death or as a longing for the purer spiritual life represented by the inspiration of Adonais. It was, after all, because Keats was a great poet, not just because he had died, that Shelley yearns to follow him.

In *Adonais* then, we can see the two sides of the poetic process. Keats's poetry had 'enlarged the circumference' of Shelley's imagination by 'replenishing it with thoughts of ever new delight', and in contemplating Keats's fate he had 'put himself in the place of another'. This is the response Shelley hopes from his own readers, firstly delight and secondly the exercise of the imagination leading to a greater good. The only 'moral' of the poem is that critics ought not, like wolves or 'obscure ravens', to feed their own vanity (and therefore self-contempt) with bloodthirsty attacks on creative spirits. (In cancelled passages from the Preface to *Adonais* we see Shelley curbing his own impulse clamorously to attack reviewers in general.) Beyond that, only the individual can judge whether he is 'better' for reading *Adonais*, whether he has come to some apprehension that 'The great secret of morals is love, or a going out of our own nature and an identification of ourselves with the beautiful which exists in thought, action, or person, not our own.' In short, whether he has shared Shelley's life-long struggle to be lifted 'out of the dull vapours of the little world of self'.

12

The Triumph of Life and Death

If there has been critical disagreement about Shelley's philosophical position in *Adonais*, there is yet more doubt about the poem he was working on at the time of his death. Understandably so, since *The Triumph of Life* is a fragment, nearly five hundred and fifty lines of 'sad pageantry', leading to an overwhelming question: ' "Then, what is life?" I cried?—'

The buoyant tone of the first forty lines is a striking contrast to the rest of the fragment. We can only guess whether at the end Shelley would have returned to the morning splendour of the beginning. As the poet watches the sunrise among the Apennines he has a vision, not, as in earlier poems, of entrancing solitudes but of a crowded public way:

> Thick strewn with summer dust, and a great stream
> Of people there was hurrying to and fro
> Numerous as gnats upon the evening gleam,
>
> All hastening onward, yet none seemed to know
> Whither he went, or whence he came, or why
> He made one of the multitude.   ll. 44–9

This multitude is incapable of feeling the influence of natural beauty, impelled as they are along the dusty highway. Soon they are overtaken by the intense, cold light of a rushing chariot driven by a blind and shadowy charioteer—power and purposelessness combined: 'little profit brings/Speed in the van and blindness in the rear.' The great of history are bound to it as captives; only a few, inspired and youthful, manage to escape. The young, dancing wildly in front of the chariot, quickly fall in its path,

like foam, 'after the ocean's wrath/Is spent upon the shore'.
The old frenziedly try to keep up:

> behind,
> Old men and women foully disarrayed,
> Shake their gray hairs in the insulting wind,
>
> And follow in the dance, with limbs decayed,
> Seeking to reach the light which leaves them still
> Farther behind and deeper in the shade.   ll. 164-9

In answer to the poet's half-spoken speculations on this dismal
dance a mentor arises. What seemed a strange, distorted root
sticking out of the hill proves to be 'one of those deluded crew',
the phantom of Rousseau, warning him against joining the
dance. He points out the notable captives, Napoleon and Plato
among them, who have finally been conquered by life, and then
he recounts his own history, how in youth he was, amidst the
beauties of nature, inspired by a 'Shape all light'; how none the
less he was overtaken by the chariot; and how he witnessed the
beauty waning from every form. So the fragment ends with the
desolation of frustrated ideals and lost hope, and the poet's
final anguished question.

The conclusion is in doubt. Despair seems near. As in *Adonais*
early death or withdrawal from the world is suggested as the
only escape from the inevitable corruption of ideals; the
fortunate:

> as soon
> As they had touched the world with living flame
> Fled back like eagles to their native noon.   ll. 129-31

But there are positives. For instance Dante (whose *terza rima*
Shelley here imitates) told 'the wondrous story/How all things
are transfigured except Love' (ll. 475-6). Perhaps this idea, central
to *The Revolt of Islam* and *Prometheus Unbound*, would have
emerged again in a completed *Triumph of Life*. Furthermore
there is the positive of the poem itself. It deals with disillusion
and suggests desolation but it confronts its themes head on, it
even examines Shelley's own heroes to see if they have feet of

clay. Though the poem is a vision, it is a public rather than a private one; Shelley gains a new detachment as he takes a historical figure for his guide. He sympathises with Rousseau, but is not identified with him. Though the advice to 'know thyself' is explicit, the search is not self-indulgent as in *Alastor*. There are passages reminiscent of that poem, for example the wood and river landscape illuminated by the 'Shape, all light' seen by Rousseau. But their radiance is contrasted with darker sections. The lines already quoted give a fair indication of the strength of Shelley's new plainer style. It says a lot for his maturing technical skill that he can incorporate into this graceful lines such as:

> And still her feet, no less than the sweet tune
> To which they moved, seemed as they moved to blot
> The thoughts of him who gazed on them; and soon

> All that was, seemed as if it had been not;
> And all the gazer's mind was strewn beneath
> Her feet like embers; and she, thought by thought,

> Trampled its sparks into the dust of death;
> As day upon the threshold of the east
> Treads out the lamps of night, until the breath

> Of darkness re-illumine even the least
> Of heaven's living eyes—like day she came,
> Making the night a dream.

Terza rima, notoriously difficult to manage in English because of the paucity of rhymes in the language, is in this poem an apparently effortless verse form for combining narrative and description, plainness and lyricism, the grotesque and the beautiful. Shelley's visions are more convincing here than in earlier poems because this mingling of effects is characteristic of most people's dream experiences, which frequently alternate between haziness and extreme clarity, as in, for example, Shelley's realisation of the figure of Rousseau. The fragment is the most compelling of Shelley's narratives.

The ambiguity of *The Triumph of Life* mirrors the ambiguity of the last year of Shelley's life, with its new friendships and projects, and its renewed distresses. Even the final catastrophe that overtook him is mysterious: was the boat, the *Don Juan*, deliberately rammed by thieves, or left to founder because of Italian quarantine regulations? Or did it capsize in a squall because it was badly designed, or because Shelley and Williams were foolhardy, putting out to sea in adverse weather conditions when they were incompetent sailors?

Amongst the distresses of 1821 were disillusionment with Emilia Viviani, the death of Keats, a degree of alienation from Mary, and difficulties over Claire. As Byron told Shelley, the accusations by ex-servants about Shelley and Claire—not only that they were the parents of the Neapolitan child, but also that they had together ill-treated Mary—had gained ground through the consul at Venice. Mary wrote to the consul's wife refuting the charge, and declaring that Shelley was 'as incapable of cruelty as the softest woman'. Meanwhile Claire, who for a time had had a teaching post at Florence, joined them again in Pisa and became increasingly agitated about Allegra. In 1822 Shelley deterred her from schemes to regain custody of her child, but Claire's fears about Allegra's well-being in the convent to which she had been consigned were justified; she died in a typhus epidemic on 19 April, 1822. At the time Claire was away with the Williamses, looking for a house for them all by the sea for the summer. Shelley, determined that she should not have to bear news of the loss in Pisa, where Byron was, sent her off with Mary and the baby Percy to San Terenzo, near Lerici, where a house was vacant.

Mary, pregnant again, found the cramped and isolated house depressing and the local inhabitants repellent, even if the situation, overlooking the shore, was one of 'surpassing beauty'. Though she too had grown fond of Jane Williams, she felt cut off from society. Shelley confessed in a letter to Gisborne in June 1822 that he felt that Mary did not understand him, and Trelawny recalls a comment Shelley made the day he wrote *With a Guitar, to Jane*: 'Poor Mary! Hers is a sad fate . . . She can't bear solitude nor I society—the quick coupled with the dead.' Though there was the pleasure and excitement of the arrival of the boat

Shelley and Williams had ordered, the atmosphere near Lerici was at least partly one of foreboding. In June Mary miscarried and would probably have died had it not been for Shelley's prompt medical treatment. But the strain told on him. As after Allegra's death, when he 'saw' her on the beach, he had visions, being convinced that he had seen his own wraith which asked him 'How long do you mean to be content?' A sense of pleasure blighted is revealed in his last sad note to Jane: 'How soon those hours pass, and how slowly they return to pass so soon again, and perhaps for ever, in which we have lived together so intimately, so happily.'

However for Shelley there *was* happiness that summer. By the middle of June it was very hot and Mary tells us that 'extreme heat always put Shelley in spirits'. The *Don Juan* had been delivered on 12 May, and as Williams said they now had a 'perfect plaything for the summer'. Even Mary enjoyed short trips in the calm of the bay, though Trelawny warned them that the open sea was a different matter. On 1 July with Charles Vivian, the boy they had engaged as seaman, Shelley and Williams set off to Leghorn to meet Leigh Hunt and his family. Shelley wanted to see them settled at Pisa, and to smooth relations with Byron who by this time was less keen on the periodical project and less than courteous to Mrs. Hunt. Mary was full of foreboding as she saw them leave, calling them back more than once. So Shelley was anxious to return quickly. He himself was, according to Mrs. Mason, on whom he called in Pisa, 'in better health and spirits than she had ever known him'. On 8 July at noon, though the weather was unsettled they set sail for home. At three their sailor-friend Captain Roberts, who had advised delay, anxiously saw the boat disappear in the mists of a violent squall. Nothing more was seen or heard of them, despite Trelawny's intensive investigations, till 18 July. On that day Shelley's body, washed up on the beach, was identified by a copy of Sophocles in one pocket and of Keats in another. Because of quarantine regulations the bodies of Shelley, Williams and Charles Vivian were buried with quicklime on the shore where they were found, some miles apart from each other. Later, so that Williams's ashes could be taken back to England, and Shelley's could be buried at Rome near his son, permission was obtained for them to be cremated. Trelawny organised the two funerals on the sea shore. A copy of Keats's poems made part of Shelley's pyre. For reasons of hygiene but also to accord with ancient custom, salt and frankincense, oil and wine were poured on his body. The flame burnt, said Leigh Hunt, 'as though it contained the glassy essence of vitality'. Byron swam away from the beautiful and terrible sight to his boat moored out at sea; Hunt stayed in his carriage; Trelawny rescued Shelley's heart, mysteriously unconsumed, from the flames.

So while he left images of enduring life imprinted on the minds of his friends, Shelley got rid of the body, and the 'burr that will stick to one', the self.

Further Reading

WORKS

Shelley: Poetical Works, edited by Thomas Hutchinson (Oxford University Press, 1967).

Shelley's Prose, or The Trumpet of a Prophecy, edited by David Lee Clark (Albuquerque, University of New Mexico Press, 1966). This edition does not contain the two early romances, *Zastrozzi* and *St. Irvine*, which will be found in *The Complete Works of Percy Bysshe Shelley*, edited by Roger Ingpen and Walter E. Peck, 10 vols. (New York, Charles Scribner's Sons, 1926–30).

The Letters of Percy Bysshe Shelley, edited by F. L. Jones, 2 vols. (Oxford University Press, 1964).

A Lexical Concordance to the Poetical Works of Percy Bysshe Shelley, compiled by F. S. Ellis (Bernard Quaritch, 1892).

LIFE

White, N. I., *Shelley*, 2 vols. (Secker and Warburg, 1947). The standard biography.

Accounts by Shelley's contemporaries include:

Hogg, Thomas Jefferson, *Life of Shelley*.

Peacock, Thomas Love, *Memoirs of Shelley*.

Trelawny, Edward John, *Recollections of the Last Days of Shelley and Byron*.

These three accounts are reprinted in *The Life of Percy Bysshe Shelley*, edited by Humbert Wolfe, 2 vols. (Dent, 1933).

Hunt, Leigh, *Byron and his Contemporaries*.

Medwin, Thomas, *Life of Shelley*, edited by H. Buxton Forman (Oxford University Press, 1913).

In addition, a caricature of Shelley appears in Peacock's *Nightmare Abbey*, under the name of Scythrop.

Two recent critical biographies are:

Cameron, K. N., *Shelley: The Golden Years* (Harvard University Press, 1974).

Holmes, Richard, *Shelley: The Pursuit* (Weidenfeld and Nicolson, 1974).

CRITICISM

Baker, Carlos, *Shelley's Major Poetry: the Fabric of a Vision* (New York, Russell and Russell, 1961).

Blunden, Edmund, *Shelley: A Life Story* (Collins, 1946; Oxford Paperbacks, 1965).

Brailsford, H. N., *Shelley, Godwin and their Circle* (Oxford University Press, 1913).

Cameron, K. N., *The Young Shelley: Genesis of a Radical* (Gollancz, 1951).

Eliot, T. S., 'Shelley and Keats' in *The Use of Poetry and the Use of Criticism* (Faber, 1933).

Hughes, A. M. D., *The Nascent Mind of Shelley* (Oxford University Press, 1947).

King-Hele, Desmond, *Shelley, His Thought and Work* (Macmillan, 2nd edition, 1971).

Leavis, F. R., 'Shelley' in *Revaluation* (Chatto and Windus, 1936).

Index to Shelley's Works

General Index